ADVANCE WORD:
THERE'S NOT AN APP FOR THAT

"*There's Not an App for That* is easy to read and hard to forget. For most of us in business and all of us in relationships, effective communication is critical. Cary reveals to us that the key to effective communication is not the message that is sent, but the message that is received."

—John C. Jarosz, Economist and Testifying
Expert Witness

"Cary Pfeffer is one of the sharpest communication experts I know and *There's Not an App for That* should be required reading for anyone hoping to lead in business and life."

—Doug Ducey, Arizona Governor and former
CEO of Cold Stone Creamery

"Cary's insight helps us identify successful communication skills and, with simple clarity, he shares how to 'get to the good stuff' immediately. Cary has not only mastered this in his own life but has coached and delivered these skills to many."

—Shauna Forsythe, President and CEO, Alliance
Airport Advertising

"Engaging, enlightening and sound advice for executives, leaders and those working to improve their communication skills."

—KATHLEEN H. GOEPPINGER, PH.D. PRESIDENT AND CHIEF EXECUTIVE OFFICER, MIDWESTERN UNIVERSITY

"Whether you are an experienced speaker or a nervous novice, this book will make you better. Cary Pfeffer has distilled many years of C-level counsel to clear, practical advice for anyone who needs to deliver an important message."

—JOHN HATFIELD, VICE PRESIDENT OF COMMUNICATIONS, ARIZONA PUBLIC SERVICE

"Cary is a genius when it comes to communicating with others. What's more, his story is inspiring. *There's Not an App for That* prepares us for interactions with business associates, employees, family members and friends."

—MIKE PENDERGRAFT, FOUNDER AND CEO, AMERICAN VALET

"Your verbal communications are crucial. When you write/text/tweet you compose, tweak and amend before you hit 'Send'. But, when you speak, it is out there. Bold, bald and irretrievable. Cary's guidance is golden! What to say, and not. When to say it, and not. How to say it, and not. Fun to read. Essential knowledge. Priceless advice."

—PETE AGUR, CHAIRMAN, THE VANALLEN GROUP

THERE'S
NOT
AN
APP
FOR THAT!

Communication Skills to BECOME
an Irreplaceable LEADER

CARY PFEFFER

Print ISBN 13: 978-1-63489-020-5
e-book ISBN 13: 978-1-63489-019-9

Library of Congress Control Number: 2015958998

Printed in the United States of America
First Printing: 2016
20   19   18   17   16   5   4   3   2

Cover and interior design by James Monroe Design, LLC.

Wise Ink, Inc.
837 Glenwood Avenue,
Minneapolis, Minnesota 55405

wiseinkpub.com
To order, visit itascabooks.com or call 1-800-901-3480.
Reseller discounts available.

This book is dedicated to my mom, dad, son, and two daughters—it all starts and ends with them.

CONTENTS

PART THREE:
Some Technical Suggestions

PART FOUR:
The Simple, Overlooked Skills

INTRODUCTION

You make a deal when you pick out a book: You'll put in the time to read *if* the author delivers a good experience. **I get that.** If you give me some of your precious time, I promise to deliver great comprehensive advice, quick tips, and specific strategies you can apply right away in your life. (Oh, and there will be a few amusing stories along the way—like the weird thing that happened to me with Penn and Teller on live TV.)

Sound good? I hope so.

What's this book about?

Technology has changed and advanced the world—while simultaneously putting people out of work and scaring another entire segment of the population. *Is my job next? Are they going to do away with our office/ shop/division?* One purpose for this book is to provide you with **the skills technology** can't **replicate**. If you improve in the areas that can't be replaced by a phone app, you also improve your chance of staying relevant in a world that is always changing.

Then there is the second purpose for this book: **People skills**. You've heard these words before. They usually sound something like this: "I wish Kevin could do something about his people skills. He's so bright and could have a great future here, but he'll need to work on the ways he interacts with people." Or people talk about your people skills in contrast to other skill sets: "Mia is a 'numbers person,' which is great, but to move ahead she'll have to brush up on her people skills."

There's Not An App for That is your resource for expertise that is not often taught or shared in the workplace or in a college class. How do you connect with others at work in a meaningful way? Why are some people better at small talk or creating a positive team atmosphere? Who can make a presentation that won't bore potential customers? And how can we get to a place where people from diverse backgrounds can be productive together—and maybe even happy?

Understanding this particular skill set has been my life's work. Effective communicators always know their audience. My entire professional career has been about reading an audience. In my early twenties, I was working fulltime in crazy, fast-paced commercial radio. By twenty-five, I was on to the even more competitive world of television news as a reporter and anchor. After twenty years and a few awards, including an Emmy, I decided to try my hand as an advisor to business leaders, actors, and athletes. The communication consulting world and television news business took me around the globe and into the inner circles of decision makers in many industries and endeavors—some of whom you know by name and will read about in this book.

And what did I learn? It's still about connecting with people. From the former mayor of New York City to the king of late night TV, it's about knowing your audience. From the lettuce growers in western Arizona to one of the largest airplane manufacturers in the world, if you don't know how to connect, you won't know how to grow your business.

On an individual basis, you won't be able to grow your career without sharpening this skill set. To put it bluntly, people get hired for their résumé—and they get fired for their behavior. Learning the skills in this book will help you to be the one getting promotions, customers, and opportunities—instead of the person watching from the sidelines.

There's Not An App for That is set up to provide you with quick, immediately useful advice that will make it easier for you to tell your story, have a critical conversation, or give a speech. You'll also learn about *looking and sounding* the part so your audience will believe you and connect with your message.

My goal is for you to **get great** at this stuff as quickly as possible, so each chapter will end with a **Get Great Point**. Summarizing the lessons of the chapter, you can count on clear direction with every **Get Great Point.**

A couple of final notes: When I mention a "talk" anytime in this book, I'm not always just referring to a speech. You can insert "conversation," "networking event," or "job interview" as well, because the rules for any critical conversation are often the same in my world. Also, the material in this book has been gathered, researched, edited, and rewritten from more than one hundred **Monthly Memos** I have written for clients over a ten-year period. The lessons referenced are real-life examples, many gathered directly on behalf of my work with clients. Finally, just in case you were wondering, my last name, Pfeffer, is pronounced Fehffer; the "P" is silent and the "e" is soft, not sharp. Just thought you might be wondering.

Get ready to boost your skills in areas where the rule book isn't always clear!

PART ONE:

FIRST IMPRESSIONS

WHAT YOU CAN LEARN RIDING ON AIR FORCE ONE

Okay, I was supposed to have this communication thing down, but as I stood at thirty thousand feet outside the conference room door on Air Force One, the only thing I could think was, *Don't screw this up!*

On the other side of the door, President George H.W. Bush was ready to record an interview; all I had to do was ask some questions. Simple, right? Except he'd already been asked everything under the sun during this election season and probably wasn't going to be too excited about being interviewed by yet another reporter.

The door swung open. The first words I heard came from the campaign press secretary, Torie Clarke: "You better watch it, Mr. President, this guy's going to be trouble." And then I heard myself saying, "Well, if you're taking *her* advice you *both* might be in trouble!" Boom. We were off to the races with laughs all around.

Okay, the laughs did stop. Especially when we got to the questions about why the president's campaign was not getting traction while running against a relatively unknown governor from Arkansas, but generally it all worked. Whew.

It was October of 1992, and I was the political reporter for the NBC TV station in Phoenix, Arizona. As the son of a bricklayer, I was hardly a likely candidate to be hanging out with the president. No one in my family had ever even gone to college before my older brother, Craig, blazed the trail. Humble, working-class background? Yep, I know all about that. And I couldn't be happier about it, because that background has helped me every step of the way.

You see, I had two advantages aboard Air Force One that day.

First, my dad, the bricklayer, taught me how to connect with people from all backgrounds. President, laborer, waitress, famous actor, student, gardener, professional athlete—by word and action, he taught me to approach each as an individual. Not better, not higher, not lower, not less than. Think of it this way: If you see a fellow employee and it's obvious that she's fair and respectful to *everyone* she meets, she automatically goes up in your estimation. She stands out. It's proof the little things matter. It's a simple lesson a humble bricklayer can teach you—and when he does, it sticks with you.

My second advantage that day was Torie Clarke; she was a friend I had known for many years. In the mid-1980s, Torie was the press secretary for a little-known Arizona congressman named John McCain. On that day aboard Air Force One, Torie was handling all of the media interaction for the president. Having someone I knew standing next to the president and warming up the meeting made all the difference.

So who are your real friends, fans, or door-openers? No, not the people you occasionally connect with online. I mean your REAL people. If you haven't made a list, make one now. These should be people who both know you well and have a strong belief in you. It can be a list of three, or, if you're lucky, a list of thirty. (Any more than that and you're probably kidding yourself!) Now that you have the list, ask yourself: *What have I done for* them *lately?* If they really are your people, you should let them know you appreciate them. It's not just the right thing to do; it also makes asking them for something A LOT easier!

Not sure *how* we are connected is important? Research shows our bonds may be keys to our overall health—not to mention our ability to perform better at work. Scientist Matthew Lieberman talked about the topic with *Scientific American* magazine in an article called "Why We Are Wired to Connect" from October 22, 2013:

> *Across many studies of mammals, from the smallest rodents all the way to us humans, the data suggests that we are profoundly shaped by our social environment and that we suffer greatly when our social bonds are threatened or severed. When this happens in childhood it can lead to long-term health and educational problems. We may not like the fact that we*

are wired such that our well-being depends on our connections with others, but the facts are the facts.

So what lesson can be learned from riding on Air Force One? Well, you can be at thirty thousand feet talking to one of the most powerful people on the planet, and the rules don't really change.

In fact, presidents and other noteworthy folks often appreciate it when they are treated like "normal" people because it doesn't happen very often. A laugh, sincere small talk, or a thoughtful answer to a question can go a long way when everyone else is just trying to get on their good side. I've had several high profile CEOs say to me, "Please, I need you to tell it to me straight, because a lot of people just tell me what I want to hear." I'm a smart aleck at heart, as is Torie Clarke; that didn't change, even though we were in the presence of the president of the United States. He appreciated it.

The *Get Great* Point

It's the human connection that makes all the difference. I would suggest that today, when we interact more often with *screens* than we do with real *people*, getting better at and valuing the human connection really is the missing link. In the coming pages, we'll talk about incorporating that vital human connection in your work world—in conversations formal and informal—and even when you're just sending an email or text.

If implemented correctly, the payoff is immense!

NEVER SIT DOWN
IN THE LOBBY

Controlling the First Few Seconds

This is a chapter about first impressions, and it starts with a very practical piece of advice: NEVER sit down in an office lobby or waiting room or any place where you're about to meet someone for the first time. Never find yourself struggling to get up from a cushiony chair that sits eight inches off the floor while the person you are here to meet stands over you with his or her hand out. ALWAYS be standing so that you can meet the person at his or her level.

While you are patiently waiting for the introduction, look out the lobby window, check out the art, or find some other excuse to remain standing, even if the person handling the gatekeeper role has invited you to sit down. "Thanks, I'm good. Just sat for an hour getting here. Need to stretch my legs." Whatever works, just don't sit.

If you're meeting at a restaurant, wait in the entryway or sit at a table facing the door so you have a clear path to stand and meet them well before they approach. If you use a wheelchair, remove yourself from the table or any interfering piece of furniture so they can meet you straight on.

First impressions matter.

How much? Ask Ned Kelly.

Kelly is VP of sales for a division of the giant Arrow Electronics. He could have chosen an office anywhere in his building, but he purposely moved into an all-glass former conference room right off the front entrance. Why? **He can see every person he is meeting with from the time they get out of their car in the parking lot.** He has sized them up before they even enter the building. The first time I visited him, I had barely said hello to the receptionist and he was already standing behind me with his hand out. Boom.

Think Ned is the only one paying attention to the details? Try this one on for size.

Done Before They Started

My colleague Elaine Kanelos told me the story of an architectural team who showed up to interview for a big project. As they approached the building, it was clear the two main architects didn't know each other. When they shook hands in the parking lot their body language betrayed the fact they were meeting in person for the first time. The team was already out of the running for the job before the first hello.

Without knowing it, they were being watched by the executive who was the decision maker for the project. (That same executive would always ask the office receptionist, "What did the team talk about while they were waiting?") The architects came in portraying themselves as a unified team, completely in sync. That storyline didn't hold up with the scene that had played out in the parking lot moments before.

Anytime you are communicating on ANY level, you need to have a strategy. As we used to say in my broadcasting days, "You are on"—even when you might not realize it. It's true for all of us.

Maybe even while you're in the parking lot.

Just How Fast Do People Make Up Their Minds?

Some of the research indicates we decide in about a QUARTER OF A SECOND! Think that sounds unlikely? Try this exercise. Next time you are in an airport concourse, on a busy street, or at a crowded sports event, look at the faces coming at you. With just a glance, you come to conclusions about people you've never met and may never see again. *Looks lost. Weird hair. Nice eyes. Too skinny. Looks smart. Where did they get that hat?* These are all examples of fast conclusions you might make about people in a split second. Do you think people are *not* doing that with you? Don't kid yourself. Clothes, body language, attitude, and posture all count more than they should; but that's just the way our brains work. We judge. Quickly.

There have been a myriad of studies done on first impressions, but one of my favorites was cited in Malcolm Gladwell's book *Blink*. A group of college students was asked to watch three ten-second silent video clips of professors; afterward, they were asked which of the three professors they preferred. With little thought, the students came to their conclusions, and their decisions were recorded. Other students came in to do the same simple assignment. As the study progressed, psychologist Nalini Ambady started to shorten the clips—eventually showing the students just two-second silent clips of the professors. Each time the students rendered their opinion, the results were recorded.

At the conclusion of the study, the results were compared to the satisfaction surveys handed in by students who had actually attended the classes the professors taught. **The results from the research study and the students who attended the class came out essentially the same!**

Gladwell summed up the results this way: "A person watching a silent two-second video clip of a teacher he or she has never met will reach conclusions about how good that teacher is that are very similar to those of a student who has sat in the teacher's class for the entire semester."

Two seconds!

So whether you subscribe to the quarter-of-a-second rule or think it might take a full two seconds to form an impression, you get the idea.

The *Get Great* Point

If you truly want to **Get Great,** you can't wait until twenty minutes into a conversation, speech, or written report to "get to the good stuff." First impression considerations should permeate everything you and your team members or colleagues think about if you are having an important interaction with anyone. (This will also help shorten meetings.)

In upcoming chapters, we'll look at how your clothing, body language, and the way you begin a speech should be a big part of how you keep first impressions in your strategic-communication planning. But first . . .

ON BEING AWKWARD

Sometimes the first impression can feel pretty uncomfortable.

During a tour through New Hampshire in 2012, presidential candidate Mitt Romney put on what has been called an "awkwardfest." Of course, Mr. Romney may have made a fine president—I take no sides on that question—and if awkwardness stopped people from inhabiting the highest office in the land, I think we would have disqualified some of our best known presidents! But I always learn something from watching public figures, and the former Massachusetts governor provided me with a case study in the socially uncomfortable. Laughing nervously, not knowing what to say next, and not always knowing how to put people at ease are all ways Mr. Romney struggled in his campaign.

Are you that awkward person at times? Is your boss? Are there embarrassing silences after certain comments? Do you hear an occasional "Ooohhhh" after a poorly timed aside? How about the struggle to make small talk? And then there's just a general discomfort in your own skin. Well, the reality is we ALL feel that way sometimes, but some people seem to be magnets for that awkward behavior. If you're one of those people, these next few tips are especially important.

"Oops, I shouldn't have said that!"

We all know the pained awkwardness of the errant comment that falls flat, or worse, offends someone. Often, the reasoning behind this is a weak attempt to be funny. Here's a tip: if the attempt to be funny preys on another group of people, it's best to just stay away. As you'll see in a later chapter, "Humor: Why Only Two Kinds of Jokes Actually Work," it's fine to make fun of yourself, but stay away from making comments that lead you down roads you should not travel!

"Gee, what should I talk about?"

The awkward among us often complain about not knowing what to say, but we've all have that sensation on occasion. If you're struggling to come up with conversation topics, the best thing to do is to keep the focus on listening and inclusion. Keep the conversation rolling by showing interest in those around you. "Tell me about yourself." "What is your connection here?" "What do you think about this meeting/issue/current event?" "Tell me more." These are all useful questions and comments to keep in mind.

The most impressive leaders with whom I work regularly are those who walk into the room as the CEO and walk out as a regular, relatable person. Of course there are times when a CEO has to take charge, but there are plenty of times when he or she can set a great example by putting others first, asking questions, and listening.

"I just always feel uncomfortable in public."

Have you tried talking to your doctor about it? Seriously, more than once I've advised clients to get some help with generalized anxiety. There are manageable options out there, especially when preparing for a big meeting or presentation. In its most serious form, awkwardness is actually a condition known as social anxiety disorder, and WebMD reports that more than 19 million Americans suffer from the malady. If you feel your discomfort may be more serious than the usual nerves, ask about it; it can only help.

The *Get Great* Point

If you've seen yourself or colleagues in these quick examples, keep in mind that the number of people nodding their heads in agreement while reading this chapter is higher than you think. What does that tell you? It tells you the awkward moment finds us all. It's completely natural to be uncomfortable and to mess up every once in a while—the important thing is to remember that you aren't alone. Just knowing that every other person in the room has been there does wonders for controlling nerves.

YOU'RE ALWAYS IN UNIFORM

First Impressions and the Clothes You Wear

Any fan can tell you the details of his or her favorite team's uniform. Packers' green and gold, Yankee pinstripes, or the Lakers' purple and yellow are recognizable in an instant to the teams' fans. But you have a uniform as well, even though you may not think of it that way. Let's see if you can picture these uniforms in your mind's eye:

For Bill Gates, it's the blue open-collar business shirt and dress pants, occasionally with a jacket. The president, any president, is usually in dark blue business attire for official duties. Then there is the "I'm letting my hair down" uniform, which is worn with greater ease. Maybe it's the jeans-and-casual-yet-dressy-shirt uniform. Martha Stewart always has the seasonal theme going in her uniform, often with a sweater draped strategically over her shoulders. And Katy Perry has a uniform plan, even when what she's wearing has been "thrown together."

Maybe you're still skeptical. Perhaps you're just not a "clothes person," or you think it's unfair that people make judgments simply based on what you chose to put on this morning. Fair enough; just remember the way our brains work and the research in the previous chapter. You may not think this way, but a lot of other people do. What's more, those people often have a say in what we do and where we go in our careers.

Think of it this way: If you're the hiring manager, police detective, loan officer, boss, or teacher, you are called upon to make decisions about people all the time—and you almost always have to do it with **incomplete information.** So, what do you do? You find short cuts—quick ways to help you with the decision-making process. What's an easy-to-use short cut? Use the way someone dresses as a partial-basis for your decision. Don't like it? Too bad; it's the way the world works.

So, what's YOUR uniform?

The Impact of Your Presentation

Anytime I'm coaching or training someone, I keep coming back to the theme, *You're on. You're always on.* It's a great way for people to remember that they are a constant living, breathing, walking representative of their gender, race, profession, faith, employer, and family name. We've already talked about the parking lot story, but I usually say you're "on" from the time you get up until the time you go to bed.

If you think of it in those terms, you realize the uniform you choose makes a big difference. People are judging you all the time, often without exchanging words with you. It may not be fair, but it is true. That equation is multiplied a thousand times when you are in front of an audience or a TV camera. (After spending more than twenty years in broadcasting, you can understand I learned this lesson many times over.)

The Basic Rules of the Road

First, you have to get over the idea that this is about VANITY. That's not what I'm talking about; I'm not talking about endlessly primping in front of a mirror or blowing your budget on a closet full of expensive clothes.

What I am talking about is *thinking* about the clothes you wear, especially in the workplace and especially in an era where casual dress is more and more accepted.

Let's face it. Certain industries are setting new rules. Tattoos and the very latest hairstyles aren't just okay; they've become the NEW uniform. If you asked many of the folks who work in tech, for example, they would tell you they don't go by any rules. No stuffy suits and ties, right? Or if it's a suit, it's the one with the latest fashion flair.

Well, I would say they are just setting up a new set

of rules, which comes with a uniform expectation just the same.

So, whether you work in an industry where your dress code is relaxed (tech, fashion, or entertainment, for example) or formal (law, banking, and most corporate headquarters), pay attention to the fact that there IS a uniform and you are going to be judged by your ability to understand what's going on around you.

If you're the boss, know you're setting a tone and sending a message with the way you dress. What is your expectation from those who work for you? Do you want them to take work seriously? Are discipline and structure important for the work you do? Are you often in contact with your customers, and do they come to you with certain expectations?

Just as legitimately, is it important for the team to feel a sense of independence? Is creativity key in your atmosphere? Will flexibility in dress code affect the optimum level of productivity? And what is the age range of your employees? Given their salary, how much can you expect them to be spending on clothing? All of these questions should be considered when deciding dress code.

If you're an employee, pay attention to what's going on around you and don't discount it. Pay attention to the way your clothes reflect your work quality and the place you hold at work. My advice is to invest in decent-quality clothes that give you a more put-together look than you might otherwise accomplish. That doesn't mean you have to break the bank investing in the latest fashion; it means you should wear clothes that look good on you and inspire confidence in you. Your actions certainly count, but don't forget how external factors play a part—a big part—in our decision-making process.

If you're one of the younger people in the workplace or one of the newest hires, these rules apply even more. You don't have years of experience to support your credibility; having a go-getter attitude is great, but your clothing should mimic how badly you want to be there and the quality of work you're prepared to put forth.

A quick story comes to mind from my days in the news business. For most of the 1990s, I worked in the largest local TV newsroom in the country, KCAL, located in Los Angeles. We had, as you might expect, a lot of interns from universities all over the country, all toiling away in the newsroom, getting experience, and hoping to find their way into the business at some point. In the meantime, they were also trying to score other media-related work in Los Angeles to help pay the bills.

Pretty soon I could see a pattern. Every once in a while, one of these usually casual interns would come to work in a nice dress or shirt and tie. As soon as I caught on I began to ask, out of the blue, "So, how did the interview go?" A look of shock would cross their face. "How did you know?" "Come on," I would say, "you changed your uniform."

How Do Your Clothes Make You Feel?

Finally, there is the fact that we are impacted INSIDE when we wear great clothes on the outside. Have you heard about the white coat research done at Northwestern University? A *New York Times* article on April 2, 2012, entitled "Mind Games: Sometimes a White Coat Isn't Just a White Coat" explained how study participants were asked to take part in a test, but before they began, they were directed to put on a white coat. Some were told that the coat belonged to a doctor; others were told it belonged to a painter. (No disrespect to my painter friends.)

Those who thought they were in the doctor's clothes scored noticeably better. This is part of a school of thought called embodied cognition, which says we think with our *bodies*, not just with our *brains*. Bottom line? If it's an important conversation, wear the clothes that make you feel like you're on top of the world.

The *Get Great* Point

While most of us spend a lot of time choosing the words we deliver when we're in front of an audience or during in an important conversation, we often forget about the uniform we wear and what it says about us. Too often casual Friday turns into casual Monday, Tuesday, Wednesday . . . remember to err on the "up" side of the clothing equation. Dress more formally than you might do otherwise (especially if you are one of the younger people in the workplace). Dress just above the people in your audience. They're deciding whether or not they'll respect you—dress like you're someone worthy of their respect.

And remember, this lesson still holds true even on the days when you're not making a presentation. The old adage still stands strong: "Dress for the job you want, not the job you have." Make sure your uniform is helping to move you forward, not holding you back.

BODY LANGUAGE AND UNSPOKEN MESSAGES

First Impressions, and What Your Body Is Saying When It Speaks for You

While the commercials were playing on that Los Angeles TV station where I worked, I talked with magicians Penn and Teller. Yes, Penn AND Teller. When you see the comedy/magic duo on stage, Penn Jillette is the only one to speak. On this particular afternoon, however, Teller was as talkative as could be; he discussed their Las Vegas stage show, news of the day, and anything else that happened to come up.

Until the red light came on.

When you are interviewing a guy on live TV who doesn't speak, you realize that you have an opportunity to learn something about body language that, someday, you just might want to include in a book! And body language makes a huge difference in the first-impression world.

For some reason I had thought Teller would continue his talkative ways once we were "on." The first question goes to Penn and he provides a flawless, made-for-TV answer. Thinking everything is great, I turn to Teller for the second question.

Nothing. Just the wan smile that is a staple of his part of the act. Geez! I was thinking the quiet stuff was something he only used on stage. Wrong. The silence goes on for two, three, four seconds. You don't know how long four seconds is until it fully fills up time on live TV. I may have blanked the rest of it out of my memory for my own sanity, but my recollection is Penn stepped in and saved me.

We Judge

We've already discussed how judgments are made based on clothing decisions; body language is an even stronger influencer in how people perceive you. Just like your uniform, people are always—in an instant—judging your body language, especially in comparison to the words you're saying. They are trying to figure out if the two match. If they decide the two are *not* in sync, they hit the rejection button.

Have you ever met someone and just felt something was off? Or maybe you've heard it in a dating situation: "I just don't *get* him." Or maybe it's how you've always felt about a particular politician: "I don't know, I just don't *trust* her."

But if you really want to see an experiment in body language, watch stage show entertainers. Body language manipulation is an area where Penn and Teller have a lot of experience, as does every successful singer or stand-up comedian. But Penn and Teller make for an especially interesting case study. Think about it: there are only two main people in the act, one of whom is taken out of the act by not speaking.

Or is he?

When you think about the Penn and Teller act, what comes to mind? If you have even the slightest passing knowledge of it, you're likely to say, "Oh, yeah, it's the one where that one guy never says anything, right?" Teller's lack of speech is their calling card.

They also demonstrate the *power* of someone never saying a word. We pay attention to Teller precisely because he isn't saying anything. His language is physical—the shrug of his shoulders, his bewildered look, his passive smile say it all—but it's amazing how much it speaks to us.

Are You In Sync?

It's the question people are constantly asking themselves, often without actively thinking about it: *Do I believe what this person is saying and do I connect with them? Are we in sync?* How do they make that judgment? Mostly, it comes down to body language—more so than the facts, charts, or research you may be talking about. Are you congruent? The issue of congruency is part of the work of the much-noted UCLA Professor, researcher, and author Albert Mehrabian.

You may have heard of his work before: When someone points out that more than 90 percent of the message you communicate is **nonverbal**, they're quoting Mehrabian. You've probably seen this statistic, too: you comprehend 7 percent of the message through the words, 38 percent from the tone of voice, and 55 percent from body language. I often use these stats as well, and I've come to understand them much more clearly over the years. Dr. Mehrabian points out those numbers shouldn't be assumed to be applicable in all situations, though, and I completely agree.

The point of this research and other research on the topic is to **not fall in love with the words** and assume that they'll carry the full load of your message. When you hear people complain about not "getting it," you might ask yourself, *Are we just telling them?* If that's all we're doing, we can't be surprised if they don't get it.

The real lesson in Mehrabian's work is that you must SOUND and LOOK like you mean it when you're communicating something of importance. Humans are always looking for that congruent message. Are our words, voice tone, and body language in sync?

You can be delivering a factually sound message and still miss the audience completely. Voters, bosses, spouses, and friends have been known to choose to support an ultimately flawed course of action because the people on the winning side sounded and looked more like they believed in their message.

The Problem with Smart People

The value of in-sync body language and communication is especially important for smart people. Why? A very intelligent or well-informed person can assume, after all of his or her hard work and research, that JUST TELLING THE AUDIENCE will be enough to make the case. Surely the audience will understand, because no logical person would come to any other conclusion, right, Dr. Spock?

Ah, not so fast. This can be huge if you happen to be someone—or work for someone—who is viewed as "brilliant" or as "one of the brightest people in the company." That person's message might connect perfectly on the inside, then draw a room filled with blank stares once the messages are shared with the outside world. These people are still very smart, but they need to use more than just logic and all of that great research. They must sound and look the part. They have to muster up some of the passion and energy they feel about their material to go along with their presentation of the data.

This is in no way meant to be an effort to "dumb-down" an important message. If you have great material, fantastic. Just understand that every audience is different and they have their own lives and areas of focus. Tailor your message in a way that connects with your audience while also respecting the importance of the material. As Mehrabian would point out, your audience is always looking to see if the message and messenger are congruent.

The *Get Great* Point

If you've ever been assigned a presentation with only two days' notice, you know the power and impact of body language. Scrambling to pull something together, we often look uneasy and don't perform at the top of our game. It's a part of the world of first impressions that can't be discounted. Penn and Teller take their focus on body language to an extreme to be sure, but by doing so, they make a great point. Body language is *so* powerful—and it can be, in itself, half of their routine.

Whenever you give a presentation, it's important you put in all the smart stuff, but remember to consider body language, as well. Reciting the statistics won't get you there if your tone, gestures, and overall physical presence aren't working in your favor. That doesn't mean you have to run around and put on a big act, but you do have to seem engaged in *all* aspects of the presentation to fully connect with your audience.

"GEE, IT'S GREAT TO BE HERE . . ."

The Importance of Coming Up with a Better Opening Line

Have you ever heard someone start a speech with, "Gee, it's great to be here"? My suggestion is, from the audience, you should shout out, "Yeah, you and everyone else we've heard talk today!" Cruel? Perhaps. But geez, is there a more overused expression? Especially when it comes to presentations meant to pitch an idea or product. As you might expect, there is a better way.

Like any "crutch" expression, it's a go-to phrase for many of us because it's easy. It seems like it really means something, but in reality it's nothing but hot air. Expressions like this are used because they appear to fit so many situations, when, really, they fit almost nowhere because the words, through ridiculous overuse, mean so little.

Here's another example, courtesy of my daughter. Kelsey had a chance to work for an established tech company right out of college. She was in the communications department (insert comment about the apple not falling far from the tree). One day, she was called to a meeting but didn't know why she was there. A senior executive was getting ready to deliver a speech in front of seven thousand people and the meeting was acting as his practice session. Kelsey asked what her role was in the meeting and was told she was simply there to provide feedback.

It's important to note here that, at the time, Kelsey was one of the youngest people in the company and was the newest member of the communications team.

The practice began and the executive delivered his first line (which I have changed slightly to protect the innocent):

"Hi, my name is John Smith, from the XYZ department at the ABC Company."

At this point my daughter spoke up, saying, "I'm sorry, I'm going to have to stop you right there."

The guy wasn't ten seconds into the talk.

But, as Kelsey knew after having heard me harp on this hundreds of times during her formative years, you should NEVER start a talk with the thing everyone in the room is expecting you to say.

As with any opening, **what you say in the first thirty seconds should be purposeful, committed to memory, and an efficient segue into the rest of the communication!**

If those are the rules you live by, you won't find yourself mumbling anything like, "I'm excited to be here. . . ." Instead, you'll zero in on what will be powerful and specific to the people who are looking at you. (Examples of this coming shortly.)

Side Benefit:

There is an additional upside to having a solid, non-traditional opening for your talk: It helps with the butterflies. We all get them, but as Edward R. Murrow once said, "The professionals teach the butterflies to fly in formation!"

Having a specific beginning in mind helps you get through the first few seconds and offers a roadmap so you can make it to your first big point. If you're up there just saying the first thing that comes to mind, the first thing that will usually come to mind for the *audience* is, *When is this person going to be done?*

Options: Let's say you're there to offer a new way for the audience to look at an old problem, or you need to get this group to take a certain action. What if you've been working on this for a week, two weeks, or even a month? It happened that way, right? So why not say that? It is far more powerful to start out with, "We have been thinking about this moment for the last two weeks and it is great to finally be here with you."

Another option is to communicate specific knowledge of the audience. "We know you are concerned about the budget, and that's exactly what we've kept in mind as we prepared for today." Or if you know there is resistance to the idea, you can hit it directly. "We know not everyone is ready to embrace these ideas—heck, some of you might hate them—but we just ask that you hear us out for the next five minutes because we kept your concerns in mind when we put this talk together." (In "Standing Up to Speak," two chapters from now, I offer ten opening line options.)

That doesn't mean you shouldn't bring excitement or energy to the top of your talk. In fact, here's the take of Scott Berkun, the author of a helpful book about the business of talking for a living called *Confessions of a Public Speaker*:

> *At the moment you open your mouth, you control how much energy you will give to your audience. Everything else can go wrong, but I always choose to be enthusiastic so no one can ever say I wasn't trying hard. The more I seem to care, the more likely people in the audience will care as well.*

Never just let those first few seconds go by—you only get them once. You can indeed be glad to be there, but how else can you say it so you have a genuine connection with the audience?

The *Get Great* Point

As with any effective solution, focusing on delivering an impactful opening line is more PERSONAL and requires MORE EFFORT. That thought process is exactly what should come to mind when you hear clichés being thrown around at any time in any important talk. You should immediately ask yourself, *What can we say that will be more meaningful for the people we need to connect with? How else can we say this? Isn't there a better way to get this across?* As soon as those questions are asked, you are on your way to finding a higher plain of communication—and actually getting the results you're hoping for.

FURTHER PROOF THIS STUFF REALLY WORKS

Having spent most of my professional life around news reporters, I have learned people can be skeptical. Twice in the book I'll provide this segment, designed for those who still have questions.

How About $60 Billion in Proof?

Ruth Porat took over as Google's chief financial officer and the market responded with a $60 billion gain—the largest one-day jump for any company ever, according to the *New York Times*. Why? While it can't *all* be attributed to her addition to the Google mix, Ruth Porat had proven her value by bringing something the outside world believed was sorely needed at Google: articulate leadership and discipline.

Ruth is a Morgan Stanley and Wall Street veteran who is known for her maturity—something that made a huge difference to those watching Google closely. And how is it that Wall Street watchers expressed the difference Ruth Porat brought to the leadership team at

Google? Here's how James R. Stewart of the *New York Times* put it in his article "A Google CFO Who Can Call Time-Outs" on July 24, 2015:

> *She's only been on the job since May. But her crisp, clear delivery, quick mastery of complicated issues and mastery of 'discipline in expense management' as she put it at last week's news conference, drew an immediate chorus of raves from analysts. And the symbolism of appointing someone like Ms. Porat at such a senior level and having her lead the earnings news conference has already altered perceptions of Google as impulsive and undisciplined.*

Did you catch that? "Crisp, clear delivery, quick mastery of complicated issues . . ."

One can almost imagine the conversation inside Google, the debate over who would represent their new face. In this case, they picked the person who had been there less than six months, but who had already made a huge impact inside the company.

Isn't that what EVERY organization has to decide? And it isn't always the CEO or founder who should be appointed. Sure, Google is already an amazing success story, but it's not perfect. Far from it. It can always improve. Founders Sergey Brin and Larry Page now see what adding an articulate, disciplined, exceptional communicator to the mix means to the outside world.

It means $60 billion, the next time someone asks.

PART TWO:

BE A BETTER COMMUNICATOR EVERY DAY

INJECTING MYSTERY AND WONDER

Remembering That Time I Forgot I Was on *The X-Files*

The scene at my brother's house must have been a weird one. He and his wife were sitting in their living room, tuned in to one of their favorite shows, *The X-Files*. The new season of the show, which dealt with the strange and unexplained, included an episode called "The Trevor."

Then the weird thing happened.

Partway through the program, I showed up on the screen as a news anchor, reading breaking news about the prison escape storyline that was threaded through the show. But how was that possible? Were *The X-Files* producers playing a trick? Had the fact or fiction nature of the show taken over their brains? What the hell was going on? My brother and his wife went to bed a little uneasy that night.

The next day I received a call at work. "Were you on *The X-Files* last night?" I immediately knew what had happened. "Oh man, I am so sorry! I totally forgot to tell you I was in an episode. It was months ago and I was getting ready to move and forgot to tell you. I didn't know you watched *The X-Files....*"

And so unfolded one of the stranger interactions where my professional and personal lives collided. While working in Los Angeles, I would, on occasion, get cast as a newsperson in a TV show or movie—since that's what I actually did for a living it wasn't much of an acting stretch. No award-winning stuff, I assure you. I had forgotten to tell my brother about this specific acting stint, so it provided a nice, surreal moment when my brother and his wife just happened to stumble across the episode.

We all like a little mystery. It gets us engaged. Don't forget mystery in your communication tool kit. Too often, we make everything in the speech, presentation, or conversation so obvious it's just plain boring.

The most over-used injection of mystery in a talk comes in the form of a question. *"How many people in this room would like an extra week of vacation this year?"* Come on, really? If that question is the best you can do, you're not working hard enough. I don't mean to be too hard on the question-askers out there, but asking those basic questions has become too much of a cliché, in my opinion. If you hear it all the time, it should tell you something.

Alternatives to the Obvious

I strongly suggest you REJECT the first idea that comes to your mind when undertaking an effort requiring imagination. Why? Well, if it came to mind that easily it probably isn't a very original thought—and thus we have people saying the same thing over and over.

Alternatives to the tried-and-true can be phrases that begin with words like, "Imagine . . . ," "What if . . . ," and "Think about this . . ." You are trying to take your listener on a journey. You are asking them to engage their imaginations and put their brains in gear. Maybe we call upon a commonly shared childhood or family-life experience that also has a twist in the story. Or how about telling them something they may not have known or had forgotten? Or sharing a surprising piece of history that will help remind people others have faced these same challenges in the past?

The CEO of Cold Stone Creamery (Doug Ducey, who later went on to become the governor of Arizona) used this technique while standing in front of thousands of franchisees at a national convention. He recalled how one of the ice cream–store owners started in a lousy location with no support from others and seemed to suffer one setback after another. The popular restaurant next door was so good that the guests were full when they left and didn't stop for an ice cream treat. Weekends were okay, but weekdays were very quiet. The store didn't even make enough money in the first year to make it possible to hire employees, so the couple who owned the store (their dream business, they thought) had to work seven days a week.

After painting this bleak picture, Ducey revealed he was talking about the couple who opened the very first Cold Stone Creamery! After a lot of early struggles, the store eventually caught on and the founders were able to open a second store which then, over the years, led to a franchise system that grew to more than a thousand stores all over the world.

Sure beats standing up and asking, *Who knows the story of how this company got started?* Be comfortable with **leaving out** some of the story—allow a little mystery to creep into the audience experience. Then, when you do get around to making your point, there is a higher level of satisfaction for your audience, and they are more likely to remember your point.

Doug decided to tell that story when the company was going through growing pains and some storeowners were complaining that they didn't receive enough support. His point became obvious: *You think you have it tough? Imagine being the very first store, with no one there to support you and only the dream of owning an ice cream store to cling to every day.* It may not have answered every question, but it helped provide some perspective.

The *Get Great* Point

An element of mystery can teach us lessons and keep us engaged; popular movie storylines can add some pizazz to your message, as can a story out of pop culture or sports with a twist. Radio personality Paul Harvey did that for years through his *The Rest of the Story* series. Look around the world, expand your options, and realize you are limited only by your imagination. Study the history of the people with whom you are speaking. From a one-on-one conversation (what is this person's backstory?) to a room of hundreds, what might click for your audience? If you're looking for additional evidence of the effectiveness of adding a little mystery and wonder to your speech, just look at Mark Twain or Abraham Lincoln. They are known to this day, in part, because they were great storytellers—and mystery and wonder were part of their tool kits. Lincoln famously encouraged hard work with this twist on a famous phrase: "Things may come to those who wait, but only the things left by those who hustle." And one of my favorite Twain quotes looks at worry. It takes the listener down one familiar track, then switches directions: "I am an old man. Throughout my life I have worried about many things. Most of which never happened."

The same tricks were used every week by the producers of *The X-Files*. The quirky, switched-up storylines take all kinds of twists and turns and for nine seasons it was one of the most popular shows on television.

And, on one particular night, it took an especially weird turn at my brother's house.

STANDING UP TO SPEAK

The Six Overlooked Basics

In speaking, there are six basic steps, which, if executed correctly, can put any speaker well ahead of another. Additionally, these six help to prevent nervousness, which leads to fewer ramblings and distractions along the way. (They're also equally applicable in almost any form of communication.)

How can it be this easy, you ask? Very often, the keys to success in any endeavor are **the basics**, even though we rarely want to believe that. It can't be that simple, can it? It can. There may be a lot of other things you can do with a speech or presentation, but focusing on these six basics first will create a significant, positive difference for you right away. The key, as always, is taking the first step.

Basic #1: How do you start? As you heard in the previous chapter, you should never start with the usual cliché statements. Instead, what statement of significance or impact can you come up with in the very first words you speak? The actor Bryan Cranston, the star of *Breaking Bad,* said he knew he absolutely had to get the part of Walter White after reading the opening scene from the first script. In an interview with *Fast Company* magazine in 2013, Cranston said after reading the first page, "What the hell? It just got you right away. It was like a feeding frenzy." He was ready to pull out all the stops and call in every favor to get cast in the show, and he hadn't even read to page three! This is because the script's opening was so good that, for Cranston, it was irresistible.

When the person across from you or the people in the audience in front of you first hear you speak, they better be hearing something engaging, otherwise they're likely to just check out. Before you speak, take a moment to make sure your audience is paying attention. Use the pause to build a little anticipation—and then reward that anticipation with a great opening line. Here are ten options to get your brain moving:

"Today is the perfect day to finally get serious about . . ."

"What if, in the next three minutes, you changed your mind about . . ."

"This is the only time we can be in one room to discuss . . ."

"I am here to tell you what you know about ___ is wrong."

"The research I'm about to show you will bring a smile to your face."

"The budget process will never look the same to

you after today."

"What if your fears surrounding ___ could disappear?"

"First: follow the rules. But today, we'll also learn from the outlaws!"

"You've probably been dreading this meeting. Be ready for a surprise."

"Only one group knows the answer to our problem. You're it!"

Now it's your turn. Spend at least ten minutes coming up with a GREAT first line and don't quit until you love your choice.

Basic #2: Why less is more. Most of us think we have to make the whole case. We believe we have to show every bit of research and every side consideration. I'm here to tell you that's what the handout, booklet, book, or Internet link is for. Just give people what they need to get to the next stop, to take the action you need them to take. Burying them in the entire process, at the very least, makes you quickly dispensable! Why do they need you around anymore if you've just seemingly given them everything they need?

But in most cases, providing too many details just makes you a really boring speaker.

Most of us need outside help to accomplish this, because we are often too close to the material to be able to edit it effectively. Make a first pass at your talk or presentation and then let others provide you with feedback, focusing on areas that can be trimmed down.

A person who can give you a tough-but-fair critique is worth their weight in gold. Do yourself a favor and search out, either internally or externally, people who can help you get to the "less is more" place anytime you are getting ready for a critical conversation or speech.

Basic #3: How your audience hears you. This is going to be short but important: no matter how much effort you put into the words of any talk, **the audience will pay more attention to how you say it than what you say.** See again our chapter on body language. Never lose track of this critical rule.

Basic #4: How do you end? Most talks end with a thud instead of a crescendo. And I'm not saying you need to pull out the fireworks, either. When you finish with a line like, "That's my last slide. Any questions?" you are seriously underwhelming your audience. Just as you spent time on a great opening line, the ending message needs thoughtful attention. The research shows that one of the most memorable parts of a speech is the beginning—second only to the end. Don't blow this chance!

You can make your final line a bookend to your opening. You can ask the audience to take the logical next steps. You can offer a vision for the future. You can tell a story to make your point. Whatever you do, just don't find yourself saying, "Okay, that's it."

Basic #5: How about a Q&A? So, let's say you've taken the first four steps here very seriously. You're really ready for this talk because you have that great first line, you have trimmed the extra fat, you are paying attention to your voice tone and body language, and you have a killer close. Great! Here's the important factor you can't lose track of when prepping: many people really make up their mind during question and answer time.

What this means is that you need to prepare for that time nearly as much as you prepare for the talk itself. You have to consider ahead of time **what** questions you may face, **who** may ask them, and **how** you might answer them. Every great trial attorney will tell you they must know the answer to every question before it is asked. You should do the same. In addition, tune up your listening skills. What is the question behind the question? What do they really mean? Who are your friends in the room? Who are the skeptics? How can you be as fair and even-handed as possible while also reminding your listeners about the key points from your original talk?

Here are some answers to those questions: When you are clearly listening to your audience, you are building goodwill—even when not everyone agrees with you. Work the room before you speak; get a feel for the makeup of the group. Many times you will be able to identify those who support you and those who do not, and gauge the overall interest level of the audience. Finally, use **transitional phrases** to work your way back to your key points. Here are four examples:

"Great point. Another way to look at that idea is . . ."

"What might surprise you is . . ."

"When I talk with some of the experts, they say . . ."

"I'd like to ask you to also consider . . ."

This is not about making everyone agree with you; it's about being the fair, diplomatic leader of the discussion. You will have far more people in your camp with this approach, and you will show a respect for everyone involved, even those who disagree.

So you're done, right? Not so fast.

Basic #6: Finishing Q&A. The final point for this chapter is worth the price of the book. Seriously. Most people end Q&A with, "Any more questions? No? Okay, thank you." Cue the golf clap. The air has just gone completely out of the balloon.

Let me suggest a better way. Finish on a question that really works for you—one that gives you a chance to circle back to one of your key points—and then say these words: **"I want to be respectful of your time. Let me just take the last thirty seconds to say . . ."**

The great thing about being in front of the room, perhaps holding the only microphone, is you get to decide how to finish this thing. Don't pass up that chance. Have a strategy for ending the Q&A that will give you an opportunity to finish strong.

Perhaps you just thank them, perhaps you hit another key point, or perhaps you acknowledge the challenges in some of the questions asked and encourage everyone to work together to find the solutions. Maybe you offer additional resources for the audience to call upon or you offer to stay around to answer more questions one-on-one. Whatever route you choose, have a plan!

The *Get Great* Point

Having a roadmap like the one I've set out for you will not only help with the butterflies, it will also help you in cleanly moving from one idea to another. You will speak with clearer sentences and not stumble over nearly as many "ums" and "ahs." Cutting back on detailed points makes it easier to follow your message. And planning for Q&A will ensure that the end of your presentation has a better chance of being successful. Use these six points any time you plan a critical conversation—especially when you find yourself in front of a room filled with people staring at you, hoping you won't waste their time.

GESTURES

So What Do I Do with My Hands?

Have you ever gotten up in front of an audience and wondered: *What should I do with my hands?*

It's one of the questions I am most frequently asked when I speak with clients about presentation skills. No one wants to look like an out-of-control windmill behind the podium—at the same time, very few people want to be addressed by a mannequin.

The most surprising piece of information I can give you is that few people have to worry about being overly aggressive in their gesturing. The problem is that people don't gesture enough, or gesture awkwardly; the bottom line is this: people are simply more natural when they use their hands while they are speaking. Here are some pointers on gesturing:

First, How Do You Gesture Normally?

If you're a person who uses his or her hands all the time, great! It's part of your personality—go with it. **The most effective speakers are confident in themselves and in their methods of communication.** Cutting out your gestures would cut off one of your best tools as a communicator. Remember, your audience is judging you by the words you use, your clothing, the tone of your voice, and your body language—which, as we know, is often the most important of those.

There is research that shows gesturing makes us better speakers. A study at the University of Alberta referenced in a May 2005 ScienceDaily article, "Hand Gestures Linked to Better Speaking," found when bilingual speakers were talking in their native language, they emphasized more often with gestures. Dr. Elena Nicoladis believes the gesturing helps bring out the story for the speaker.

Often, I describe the same idea by saying gestures act like the *punctuation* for your message; other research has shown gesturing often *leads* the story, helping telegraph where you're going to your audience. Author and speaker Carol Kinsey Goman, PhD, wrote about gesturing for *Forbes* in her article "Great Leaders Speak with Their Hands" in September 2010. She says a lot rides on timing. "Although people may not be aware they are doing so, audience members are . . . evaluating a leader's sincerity by the timing of his or her gestures: Authentic gestures begin split seconds before the words that accompany them. They will either precede the word or will be coincident with the word, but will never come after the word."

I'm willing to bet, now that you think about it, you've known that all along, but you may have never realized it. Don't forget it now.

What If You Do NOT Normally Use Your Hands?

You might remember when former Vice President Al Gore and former Senator John Kerry were parodied by *Saturday Night Live* (among others) for gestures that seemed out of sync with their words, showing up a second or two *after* they had made a particular point. There are few things more uncomfortable to watch than a person who is practicing random gesturing— ill-timed flailing of the arms only distracts from the message and the messenger.

I remember interviewing Senator Kerry when he was running for president in 2004; I had recently ridden on his campaign train as it made stops across the western states. He had just accepted the Democratic Party's nomination, and he had some ground to make up on President George W. Bush.

Senator Kerry's wife had just been interviewed in *Time*. She responded to a question about his some-times-stiff appearance in public by saying if people got to know the "real John," the votes would come his way. So I asked him what he needed to do to take his wife's advice.

He responded by saying something that spoke volumes about his unsuccessful run for president, offering that people understood him just fine and connecting with people wasn't a big worry. Here's what that looked like to audiences: with every speech, Kerry spoke as if he were addressing his colleagues on the Senate floor! Basically nobody talks or looks like that EXCEPT on the Senate floor. It is a stiff, formal, completely unique way of looking and speaking, and he never could break out of it. His stiff look and gestures never revealed the "real John," and he never made any significant traction in the election. He didn't lose the race because of bad gesturing, but it sure didn't help, either.

So how do you know if you're a bad gesturer? Well, the camera can be your friend—sometimes a better friend than your real friends, because the camera doesn't hedge or soften the message. If you have an important speech or presentation, ALWAYS record yourself while practicing. The camera will tell you things you cannot possibly know by just going over the speech in your head. (Some will tell you to do the speech in front of a mirror. My rule with executives and everyone else: Use a camera. You're more natural when you can't see yourself.) It's vital that you know what you look like to the audience and how you can use all of your tools to get your message across.

Finally, if you or your bosses are prepping for a BIG presentation, get some professional help from an experienced presentation coach. You wouldn't dream of going into court on a big case without a sharp lawyer at your side. Never make the same mistake on a major presentation. And, let's see, as you consider who to bring in to prep your team, you might consider giving my office a call. Just a subtle suggestion!

The *Get Great* Point

Often people do or do not believe us for reasons beyond just our message, our fancy business card, or the famous brand that might be connected to our name. **They decide whether or not to believe us based on who we are.**

Unfortunately, people rarely get the opportunity to really know the speaker at a presentation—that's why it's so important for you, as a speaker, to concentrate on projecting who you are and how you would like to be seen. That might seem too heavy or esoteric for a business book, but it's important to keep in mind if you want to come across as sincere. People connect and believe in us for a reason, and it doesn't always come from a purely logical place.

A little detail, such as how you gesture, can loom larger than you think. Make sure your gestures are a natural extension of your message and not scripted or haphazard. It gets back to the point about **congruence** that we talked about in the body language chapter. Pull out your camera. See yourself as others see you when you speak.

Do you believe you?

When you do, it will be easier for others to do the same.

UNDERSTANDING YOUR AUDIENCE

You Can't Know Too Much About the People in Front of You

There is a young man I know who, by age twenty-three, had started a regional magazine and a small record company, fronted two locally popular bands, and was running a coffee shop/music venue. How do you explain that level of productivity from someone that age? Perhaps the coffee plays a part, but it can't be the *only* explanation. A really important part of the explanation, I think, comes from his **understanding of his audience**. And that is a lesson we can all take with us.

If you want to connect with almost anyone in this world, you must spend the time to try and figure out who they are. In the chapter titled "Say What?" we'll take a close look at **listening** skills, but for now we are looking at the bigger picture.

Not the usual starting place: Let's face it, most of the time when we want to connect with someone (get a job, a date, a sale, a promotion, or whatever) this is not our usual starting place. We're usually thinking about one person.

We're looking in the mirror.

And can you guess who the person you're trying to reach is thinking about? Well, let's put it this way: they probably didn't wake up that morning thinking about you!

Is it any wonder that we spend a lot of time frustrated, talking right past each other? What can we do to make our communication work a whole lot better? Well, you can't control what the other person is thinking, but you can control your side of the equation, and that's what this chapter is all about. In a time when face-to-screen communication is robbing us of personal interaction, spending some time getting better at understanding the people in front of you will help you get where you want to go. (And there are a lot of ways technology can help.)

This does not mean going on a weeklong retreat with every person with whom you need to connect. It may be nothing more than looking up a person's LinkedIn profile or making a call to find out more about the culture of the office you are visiting. It may mean browsing through a few websites or Googling the nonprofit this person or group is supporting. Whatever it is, make the effort.

What is a Person's Favorite Sound?

This is one of my favorite quiz questions. Do you know the answer?

Anyone's favorite sound is his or her own name. What do we all want to hear? We want somebody calling us, letting us know we matter, that we're worth the effort. It's built into who we are—from the time our family members call out to us as small children.

So, if you are meeting one-on-one with someone, know his or her name—and say it. And not just when you first meet them; include it once or twice in the conversation and always when you say good-bye. People want to hear their name, and they want to be shown that you care enough to know it. (More on this in the chapter "Say What?")

Speaking of caring: what does this person or group care about? If you don't know the answer to that question, you shouldn't be having a conversation with them. Whether it's problems at work or stressful situations at home, we all have issues that are near and dear to us. One of my favorite leaders ends each conversation with, "What can I do for you?" Just offering that question can open a door to better, clearer, and perhaps even deeper understanding.

If you are still struggling to come up with an opening line for a talk or conversation, this is a great place to start. If you wanted to get *my* attention, for example, a great and unexpected way to start a conversation with me would be, "I was so interested to learn more about

Gompers Center. I see you've been on the board there for almost ten years."

You've let me know, right from the start, that you understand the person in front of you and that you've done your homework. While there are a number of issues I am passionate about, Gompers (gomperscenter.org) is a place that has cared for people with disabilities for more than sixty-five years and is near and dear to my heart. If you know this about me, I know that you have taken the time and effort to get to know me as a person, and I'm more likely to do the same for you.

Understanding How the Brain Works

This idea of understanding your audience becomes even more pressing when we consider how the brain processes information, filtering out what it deems to be unimportant at an amazingly quick pace. With thousands of stimuli coming at us all the time, we have to filter, otherwise we would go insane.

A Stanford study called "The Nature and Roles of Attention" looked at how we regularly filter out what happens around us, focusing only on what we care about. This sifting of information is called **top-down processing.**

What is important at one moment may no longer be so at the next, and our goals shift accordingly. If you're hungry, you may notice

a basket of luscious-looking fruit on a nearby
table—but if you've just eaten, your attention
may glide right over it with barely a pause.

Did your audience just eat, or are they starving? You have to know before you begin. As they listen to you, they will always be filtering, choosing, editing your words at a rate far faster than you can ever hope to adjust to; you must know everything you can know about your audience. Researching what they care about gives you at least a chance of connecting—offering a bowl of luscious fruit when you're pretty positive they're hungry.

The Young Entrepreneur and His Audience

Now back to the young man from the beginning of this chapter. You can't launch a regional magazine and small record company, lead rock 'n' roll bands, or even run a coffee shop/music venue without knowing your audience. I've watched in amazement as these ventures have taken off and gained local attention and notoriety—and I've watched with a pretty close view, because this young man is my son, Robb. (Okay, right now you might be thinking, *Geez, another story about one of his kids?* But stick with me here.)

Whenever Robb talks about any of these ventures, he refers to his "community." It's another way of talking about his audience, and it's the millennial approach to the age-old marketing question, *"Whom are we hoping to reach?"*

Robb used these pieces—the magazine, the record label, the band representation, and the coffee shop—to build on one another. In earlier days, before he hit his entrepreneurial side, he spent two years as one of the cartoonists at his college newspaper. This is what taught him the importance of understanding your audience—you can't sell humor if your audience doesn't find it funny. Once he began to exercise his mind in that way, he found his niche. Robb launched a 'zine to provide a place for his cartoons and others' artwork. Then it was on to the coffee shop/music venue in an old abandoned space near campus. (Yes, there were a few visits from city officials, but somehow it all worked out.) Once he started to meet and get to know up-and-coming bands, his music career and the indie record label were able to get started. (All the while, he was also finishing his undergraduate degree; so yes, coffee had to have played a part.)

Framing the story in this way, we're able to get a true sense of the importance of community. None of these ventures was huge in scale, but all were built upon the foundation of reaching his community and, with each step, the community responded, and the outside world started to take notice.

The *Get Great* Point

I'm not sure where Robb's next adventure might take him, but I'm sure his unique knowledge of his audience will light the way. So, whether you are opening a coffee shop or just getting ready for an important conversation, know your audience **first.** They will appreciate your effort, and your chances for success will be greatly increased.

PACING, PAUSES, AND JOHNNY CARSON

The King of Talk Shows Still Has Something to Teach Us

There were two reporters who were allowed behind the scenes at the *Tonight Show* studios in Burbank, California, to witness the last episode Johnny Carson taped of the *Tonight Show* in May of 1992.

I was one of them. It was the luckiest day of my professional life.

Carson ruled late-night television from the mid-1960s up until his retirement in 1992. He was one of my idols growing up. His retirement designated the end of an era in TV.

So what does this have to do with your journey to **Get Great**? Well, Carson was one of the best at pacing and pauses—setting up the speed of his delivery to get the maximum effect. That is something any of us can use when delivering an important message—and all it takes is some thought and preparation.

Let's say you're getting ready to deliver an

important talk. Whether it's an official speech or something less formal, you want to have purposeful pacing. When you practice (and you DO practice, don't you?) look for maybe two times where you can **purposely pause.** You're most likely not looking for a big laugh like Carson, but strategic pausing will help immensely in keeping people engaged. (If nothing else, a few audience members will take a moment to look up from their phones. It's tough keeping people's attention these days.)

When Do You Pause?

Here are some excellent spots: When you're about to make a major point, when you're getting ready to wrap up, or when you are shifting to a new point. How about after offering something your audience wasn't expecting, or when you've introduced a new or especially complicated idea? Let it soak in. Pause.

Carson was famous for getting a laugh for the joke, then pausing and getting a second laugh just by staying quiet and letting his audience think about it. He made you feel like you were on the inside—getting the inside joke.

Too often we are focused on spitting out the points, sometimes racing along out of nervousness or through lack of confidence. A confident speaker takes her time, letting the points settle with the listener. That very characteristic is what helps distinguish an experienced speaker from a relative newcomer. The practice and discipline that come with experience often directly impact the ability of the speaker to pause—to breathe—and let the audience take in the material being offered. So if you lack the actual experience, remember to practice, practice, practice.

This rule doesn't just apply to speeches given in front of an audience of hundreds or thousands. Think about using this same technique when you are having an important one-on-one conversation. Do we rush through, or do we pause to let the other person think and react? I suggest pausing; it gives confidence to your message, which will then have a far greater impact.

Kristina Lundholm is a speech pathologist who writes about linguistics. She notes in the ScienceBlog article "Pauses in Speech" that "Pauses are necessary in communication; we need to breathe, think, and leave gaps where another person can take over. Pauses also make it easier for the listener to process and understand what we are saying."

Help with "Um," "Er," and "You Know"

There is a surprising side-benefit to pausing. If you are a person who is plagued by too many "filler" noises and phrases—the dreaded "ums" and "ahs"—a pause can very much be your friend. My crutch for a time was "you know." A senior colleague kindly pointed it out and I actively started to briefly pause instead of falling back to my crutch. Two things happened: First, I eliminated about 90 percent of my bothersome issue. Second, very simply, I sounded more thoughtful. I wasn't rushing through my points, and the audience sensed I was giving more thought to each idea I presented. What can feel like a long stretch to the speaker actually passes quickly for the listener, and you get much more credit in the process.

One other side note here: some people, bosses, and organizations can be real sticklers about these crutch sounds and phrases. Toastmasters' groups sometimes ring a bell with each "um" or "ah." I am far more flexible on this. My rule is if someone sounds authentic while also being intelligent and thoughtful, I would much rather let them throw in the occasional filler. Expecting everyone in this day and age to speak perfectly is unrealistic, and it can get some valuable communicators so far away from their comfort zones that they are actually hindering their ability.

What About Pacing?

If you are searching for a way to get people to lean in—both mentally and physically—when you're speaking, look at changing your pace. After speaking at your normal pace, make the conscious effort to slow down. Listeners will often actually lean forward because the words carry more weight. Try it. And what if you're recounting the obvious? Pick up the pace. Most everyone knows you're covering this ground because you have to, but it isn't what needs to be emphasized, and you don't want to bore your audience.

If you pay attention, you'll notice that presidents and other leaders who more often than not speak in a formal setting use pauses to their advantage. Whether you are listening to a recent example from Barack Obama or recalling a piece of history from Ronald Reagan, you can hear the pacing in action. How effective would President Reagan have been if he had raced through his line at Germany's Brandenburg Gate? If he hadn't paused before calling out, "Mr. Gorbachev, tear down this wall!" the line would have lost a lot of its impact. With years of experience as an actor before entering politics, the man knew a good line when he saw one and understood how to deliver it.

After hearing about pauses and pacing, you might wonder just how you really incorporate it all. For most of us, it's not something you can do with the flip of an internal switch. Generally, the key is practice—and by that I mean practice with someone else or at least (once again) with a camera. It's very difficult to rely on your own perspective, because when we are the speaker we know the material. None of it is new to us, so trying to really zero in on the impactful sections can be difficult. This is why practicing in front of someone is so helpful. I would even recommend practicing in front of a few people, because every audience member can react differently.

Try to take yourself back to when you first learned

about the material that you're going to present. What drew you to it? What still blows you away today? Get in touch with those thoughts, practice, and then ask for some feedback. (More on effective practice in a later chapter.)

Johnny Carson had so much practice—all of it on camera—that he delivered a masterful performance almost any given night. He would be interviewing a famous actor or just someone from main street USA, and you could practically see the wheels turning inside his head. On one particular night, for example, actor Ed Ames was asked to show off his prowess for throwing a tomahawk. Ames played Mingo on the TV series *Daniel Boone*, and the *Tonight Show* bit had Ames throwing the tomahawk at a wooden cutout of an attacker. With Carson standing nearby, Ames threw the tomahawk directly into the crotch of the wooden figure. Embarrassed, Ames quickly moved to get the weapon. Carson grabbed him, stopping him from going anywhere and, by leaving room for a pause, gained a big laugh from the audience. It gave the director time to get a close-up of the landing spot, and that drawn-out laugh ended up being one of the most memorable scenes from Carson's early years on the show.

The *Get Great* Point

Pauses and pacing are two simple tools available to us all. Don't forget the classic lessons—they just keep paying dividends. What worked for Johnny Carson, past presidents, and other memorable communicators can be borrowed, fine-tuned, and added to your tool-box. Here's the real proof: Carson borrowed the idea from the previous generation. Comedian Jack Benny was the king of the comedic pause, and when you watch clips of the two, you can see the lesson carried through time.

FURTHER PROOF THIS STUFF REALLY WORKS

For the skeptics among us, proof. And this example is especially timely as technology skills are regularly offered as the key to the future.

Consider the research and study done by Geoff Colvin. He wrote *Humans Are Underrated* and has closely looked at where we are headed in the workplace, especially focusing on technology and the place we will play alongside technology in the future. (He also authored *Talent Is Overrated*—one of my favorite business books.)

He wrote about looking forward in an article with the same title as his book, "Humans Are Underrated," in *Fortune,* where he is a senior editor-at-large:

> *Being a great performer is becoming less about what you know and more about what you're like. The emerging picture of the future casts conventional career advice in a new light, especially the nonstop urging that students study coding and STEM subjects—science, technology, engineering, math. It has been excellent*

advice for quite a while; eight of the 10 high-est-paying college majors are in engineering, and those skills will remain critically import-ant. But important isn't the same as high-value or well-paid. As infotech continues its advance into higher skills, value will continue to move elsewhere. Engineers will stay in demand, it's safe to say, but tomorrow's most valuable engineers will not be geniuses in cubicles; rather they'll be those who can build relationships, brainstorm, collaborate, and lead.

And to show you this is not a hall of mirrors, where one writer shows you only what another similarly minded writer thinks, look at what the numbers showed Colvin in **current job growth from the same article**:

The biggest increases by far have been in education and health services, which have more than doubled as a percentage of total jobs; professional and business services, up about 80%; and leisure and hospitality, up about 50%. The overall trend is a giant employment increase in industries based on personal interaction. That's why Oracle group vice president Meg Bear says, "Empathy is the critical 21st-century skill."

Are you a *"genius in a cubicle"*? Or do you work for one? The question I'm asking is, what *else* are you doing to bring value? When you look ahead by just two years, how much will have changed with that "genius" material you now rule? Ask the people at Blackberry, MySpace, and a hundred other places you've never heard of (and now never will). These people will tell you that what matters the most about their time at these once-hot companies isn't the now-obsolete technology, but the experience of contributing in their own ways, the people skills they acquired, and the relationships they made. Today, being smart is about adding to your value in ways that make a long-term difference.

How do you build relationships, collaborate, and lead? Often, it is by sharpening the very skills we are talking about in this book: eye contact, listening skills (both coming up in the next section), and the ability to express yourself—either one-on-one or in a group. Showing you can be empathetic, connect, and communicate with others isn't old fashioned—it's what will set you apart right now.

PART THREE:

SOME TECHNICAL SUGGESTIONS
(SIX WAYS TO MAKE IT EASIER TO CONNECT)

STAYING RELEVANT IN A CHANGING WORLD

A Quick Lesson from the Former Mayor of New York

Walking into the room to teach Rudy Giuliani something about dealing with the media was a bit daunting. I mean, come on, a bricklayer's son teaching the guy who led New York City after 9/11 how to do a TV interview? Sounds ridiculous. But that's exactly where I found myself in 2013.

We are in a constantly changing world, and the mindset that you are a "finished product" can quickly lead to disaster. If you understand that things are in a constant state of change, you will be okay with the idea of constantly being a student. You'll learn the value in considering different perspectives, and you might even find that you're okay with being wrong every once in awhile. That doesn't mean you walk away from your core values—you still have to have foundations in honesty, fairness, and caring. What I'm talking about here is understanding enough about the bigger picture to know there is a lot you don't know.

This is a lesson I learned while attending an all-male high school where most everyone was smarter than me. As freshmen, we were divided into quadrants—and I was in the bottom 25 percent. Guys can be known for having a bit of an ego, but I learned early on to keep all that in check. When you are regularly around people who score in the upper reaches of the top 1 percent of high school students in the country, you learn to shut up and listen. You also learn that value comes in a lot of different forms, sizes, and shapes; you also learn that it's important to recognize and embrace your own value, especially if it isn't traditional.

What Kind of Smart are You?

You need to know this. Some of us are book smart. Some have incredible intuition and can read people. Some are problem solvers and can quickly put an entire room at ease. Since those high school years, I started to realize I didn't need to know how to perform surgery, build a stadium, fly a plane, or run a company. I could help people say what they needed to say—how to word it in a way it made sense—which is a skill that I turned into a career. Many times, very bright people struggle to explain their ideas, so being in a room with more skilled, talented, famous, rich, or powerful people is all good by me, because I know that they wouldn't be as influential as they are without a little help from me. My role may not be in the spotlight, but it is crucial.

One of the most important journeys for any of us is figuring out the role we play—and then adjusting as the world changes around us. Start by reflecting on what others say about you. (I'm not talking about that mean uncle who said you would never amount to anything when you were a kid.) What do people who know you, care about you, or are knowledgeable judges of talent tell you? What do the tests that are readily available tell you? What does your heart tell you? From reading *What Color Is Your Parachute?* to visiting with people you respect, try to get to that place where you know your role and can be okay with the changing world.

What Can I Teach Rudy Giuliani?

With that, we return to that New York City conference room with Rudy Giuliani. I was there to work on some messaging with him—getting him comfortable talking about the attributes of the product for which he had been acting as a spokesperson over the last few years. Knowing his history, I assumed he would be, at the very least, skeptical about our session. But instead of giving me the, "Yeah, yeah, got it" that I expected, he was actually very engaged. Three times during the session he said, "This is great," and "This is exactly what I needed."

This guy, who has probably spent as much time in front of news cameras as anyone on the planet, short of perhaps one of the presidents (although he tried to get that job, too), also understood he was not a "finished product." He knew that each of his roles requires a certain level of preparation and serious focus. You may like or dislike Mr. Giuliani, but I came away from our session with a renewed respect for someone who was happily ready to be a student.

The *Get Great* Point

What is your natural mindset when it's time to learn? If you're like me, you get an uncomfortable feeling in the pit of your stomach. *Can I do this? Will I embarrass myself or my team? What are others thinking?* Those self-doubting moments are pretty common for most of us. Can I suggest that the even more damaging thoughts are those that tell us we have no need for new information? Make a mental note to remain a student, a learner, and therefore always know you are open to improving.

HOW TO HANDLE THE "BLANK-OUT"

We've all been there: that key moment in a conversation or speech when your mind goes completely blank. Ouch! I was amazed that at the pinnacle of his career, during his greatest Olympic triumph, swimming superstar Michael Phelps said about a dozen times, "I'm at a loss for words" right after breaking the record for individual gold medals. Really? You've been working your entire life for this moment—and knew this might happen as you prepared over the previous three years—and you don't know what to say? For a person who had spent so much time preparing in every other way, he seemed surprisingly unprepared for the situation he knew he could face.

Sometimes I think I followed my speaking and journalism career path because of a similar example—except it was my big moment in the spotlight, and I completely blew it. But we'll get into that later.

Proper prep work can set up anyone—from a celebrity to a new college graduate—for success, and it reflects well on that person. Now let me be clear, Michael Phelps is an amazing athlete—he's amazing at what he does—but he didn't make much impact with his words. It got me thinking of simple rules for handling those times when your mind just doesn't seem to be coming up with any good ideas.

Appreciation

If the situation calls for it, the quickest and easiest thing you can do when your mind blanks out is thank those who have helped you along the way to the place where you're receiving recognition. Wouldn't it have been great if Phelps would have launched into a thank you for all those coaches and others who worked with him and provided volunteer hours at those swim meets early in his career? Everyone (not necessarily by name) who was there for him and helped him reach this lofty place? All of us get where we are with the help of others. When you find yourself at a loss for words, a thank you is not only a soft place to land your blank mind, it's also highly appreciated.

Now let's take this a step further. Let's say you've been offered some not-so-welcome news. You didn't get the promotion, you're getting fired, or you're being given some other form of bad news, and you just blank out from anger or fear or shock. What then? Believe it or not, an expression of appreciation in that moment is an unexpected and often welcome sign of having your act together. Are you still angry, sad, or shocked? Sure—but you've shown yourself to be someone who can rise above your situation. Offer a quick thank you and an expression of empathy for the difficult situation of the other person, and then make a timely exit. Staying around only increases the chances for you to see the situation deteriorate, and you don't want that to happen.

Spreading the Credit and the Lessons

Another option for a quick-fill when you blank out is to demonstrate leadership by talking about what others can learn from your experience. How about if Phelps had said, "I hope anyone who is watching this can be inspired to pursue their dreams. It's not about being an Olympic gold medal winner—it's about chasing your dreams and not settling for what's easy or the boundaries someone else says you have to live within." This blank-out landing spot should never be out of reach for you; just keep in mind what the situation means for others or how you can help others by offering insight on what is happening with you.

Let's say you are suddenly offered a big-time compliment at work. Many times, we're caught by surprise when it happens, especially if it happens in front of a group of coworkers. A quick comment that shares the credit with others on your team and expands the compliment to what this means for others in your situation makes you a champion with a much bigger, and more generous, view than most. The more you make a regular habit of thinking of others and the impact they have, the easier it is to expand your thoughts in a difficult or surprising situation.

Largesse

This is the word I have on the bulletin board next to my computer in my office. This world could use a little more largesse and a little less ego and self-importance. It's unusual for an honored person to genuinely share the spotlight and show how much they care for those who have helped them. Let's change that! Let's make it the norm to offer praise for others (even the competition) and show an understanding of the journey instead of breaking an arm patting ourselves on the back. Michael Phelps was certainly humble considering the magnitude of his accomplishment, but wouldn't it have been great if he had immediately begun speaking about the amazing athletes who have inspired him over the years and therefore helped him get to this place?

Let's think of one of the most high-profile situations where people can blank-out: the Academy Awards. Have you ever seen a seasoned actor, with plenty of film credits, stand before millions of viewers and just freeze? Yep, it can happen to the best of us. (Your industry probably has its own version of the Academy Awards, and you can see the same scene play out.) Now contrast that stumbling embarrassment with the person who stands up and has the presence of mind to remember everyone *else* who was nominated and how much they appreciate the work of *those* artists. Without fail, I am impressed when anyone can do that. It is the definition of largesse, and one we can all learn from.

A *Psychology Today* article by Erika Casriel, "Confidence: Stepping Out," talks about incorporating these kinds of suggestions to help with anxiety and those "blank-out" moments, focusing on how we process what's happening to us in the moment:

> *Six studies compared two groups of people during a hair-raising event such as an impromptu speech: One group said that their bodies were freaking out and another group said they felt calm. In five of the six studies, there was no physiological difference between the two groups. Everyone showed similarly increased levels of autonomic activation, such as sweating and speeding heart rate. "People who are very socially anxious tend to pay attention to their bodies and magnify that response, perceiving it subjectively **to be much greater than it actually is**," says James J. Gross, director of Stanford University's Psychophysiology Laboratory.*

The most successful communicators are often nervous, but they have learned how to process that energy. By incorporating the suggestions I am offering in this chapter, you can set an emergency roadmap for when these obstacles occur.

My Own Blank-Out

Now to the episode that just may have led me to this line of work. I was the class representative chosen to speak at my eighth-grade graduation, and I blanked. I still remember how quiet it got in the gymnasium at my school as I stared out at the audience—which included my parents and aunt and uncle—and they stared back at me. The fact is I was overconfident and walked up there with no notes. (More on that in the next chapter.) Even at age thirteen, I had already won some speaking awards, so I thought I had this thing down cold. Wow, was I wrong. Failing at that high a level (for a thirteen-year-old) has a way of sticking with you and providing eternal motivation. I can't even recall how exactly I got out of it—hopefully I expressed gratitude to the teachers and parents and got off the stage. There have certainly been other times in my life when I have been at a loss for words, but never a situation quite like that. It leaves a mark.

The *Get Great* Point

For those Michael Phelps fans, I was right there with you in being amazed at his accomplishments. The fact is, however, very few athletes get that chance—to completely have the spotlight to themselves because of the magnitude of their feat. He needed to be ready to answer those questions as a champion. We can all learn something from this example, because we all have things for which we strive. Turn the spotlight into a chance to show character and appreciation and maturity and largesse instead of just saying, "Gee, I'm at a loss for words!"

HOW SHOULD I ORGANIZE
MY NOTES?

The key to success in almost any endeavor is preparation, and this includes speech notes. What kind of notes work best? Neat, clear, complete notes give you the best chance of success, but it really comes down to what works for you. I recall one occasion where I was emceeing an event for about five hundred people. As I finished one of my segments, I scooped up my notes and walked off, not realizing the other speakers had left their notes on the podium as well. Now their notes were mixed with mine in a wrinkled mess in my sweating hands. The silence in the room while I sorted things out for the woman speaking next, in front of the entire audience, gave me flashbacks of that eighth-grade graduation scene.

Most dilemmas that we hope to avoid can be handled by having clear and easily accessible notes. It's worth the effort. Here are some easy-to-follow suggestions to help you avoid an embarrassing scene.

The 3 × 5 Index Card

If you're speaking and you need more than a 3 × 5 index card or two, you may be covering too much ground. The classic 3 × 5 card with three or four bold, clearly written bullet points should do the job. When you speak, you should have an obvious path of easy-to-grasp ideas to engage the audience. Often, your notes tell you if you're trying to say too much. And if your topic is a tough one, it's your job to make it easier to grasp—that's why *you* are in front of the room. Also, the complicated stuff can always be covered in a hand-out, web link, video, or book that follows the talk.

Key Sentences

A sheet or card with key sentences works well, especially if you sometimes struggle to remember specific parts of your speech. The sentences (in large, clear font) jog your memory and remind you how you wanted to express important thoughts. As you practice and prepare, you'll notice certain phrases that just work, and sometimes it pays to have them down word-for-word instead of relying on your memory.

The most important point here is to not let this system morph into pages and pages of notes that have you reading a script of your presentation. Notes are meant as just that—notes. This is not a manuscript from which you read with your head down 95 percent of the time. Only in rare occasions, such as some legal settings, stock price commentary, or delicate personnel issues, should there be a script or anything close to it.

PowerPoint

Many speakers simply use PowerPoint as their script, which usually results in something that sounds like this: *"Okay, so, moving on. Let's see . . . oh, yeah. On this next slide, the point I wanted to make is . . ."* Yuck! If PowerPoint is your *roadmap*, that's fine, but you have to be very familiar with the slides so you can smoothly move from point to point. If you sound just as confused as the audience, that's a problem. Slides should have no more than three or four clear lines and hopefully a compelling, related image that underlines the message the slide is meant to communicate. The slides are simply a tool to help reinforce your message, not a wide-screen script that ends up being read word for word.

Eye contact is really the heart of all of this. If you are in front of ten people or ten thousand people, you will be judged based on your ability to maintain some level of eye contact. (The upcoming chapter, "You Talkin' to Me?" is focused on just this critical issue.) Having clear, concise notes at which you only have to glance once or twice can help you maintain eye contact with your audience.

Media Interviews

Notes are great here—just don't pull them out in the middle of a *Today Show* interview! What I mean is you can prep some notes, know your key messages, and practice, but you can't pull your notes out during an interview without doing serious damage to your credibility. The question becomes, "Do you know this stuff or are you faking it?"

Phone Calls

Phone interviews are a great time to use notes, even if you think you won't be flustered in the comfort of your own home or office. You still want to have your main points laid out (as well as responses to potential questions), and it helps to refer to your notes at the end of the conversation to make sure you covered the key points you wanted to mention. Again, clarity and simplicity are key because the person or people with whom you are speaking won't want to sense that you're simply reading off your notes. Another key to phone success? **Always stand up.** If it's a phone conversation where there is a level of substance on the line, speak standing up. Your voice will sound clearer and more energized, and you will be less likely to be distracted by all those things that can pop up on your computer screen. Smile, even though they can't see you. Your smile will come through in your voice. (Another upcoming chapter,

"What Do I Do about My Speaking Voice?" covers this vital topic.)

The *Get Great* Point

Don't be afraid to experiment with your note process when you are called upon to speak or as you prepare in order to find that system that works best for you. The overall goal is to work with notes that keep you on track, provide the material you need, and make it possible to maintain that all-important eye contact.

And never walk away from a podium with someone else's notes!

SHOULD I STAND TO SPEAK—AND WHERE?

Often, in answering the question about what I do for a living, I say, "I help people when they stand up to speak." Of course, as has been mentioned to me many times, not everyone STANDS when they speak. But, generally, you should. Not only does your voice sound better and carry more, you can also maintain eye contact with everyone in the room more easily. And, because you are the only one standing, you become the largest presence in the room; to put it simply, standing up gives you an aura of authority.

To Stand or Not to Stand?

If the meeting is a roundtable discussion meant to be intimate, I think most of us would agree it would seem out of place to suddenly jump up and start speaking. You also need to consider the culture of your workplace. Are you in a place where nobody stands to speak? Some places are exactly that way. This offers two different options for you: go with the flow, or be the person who breaks the mold. It's not always bad to take the chance to stand out. And be aware that trends are changing in office culture. Many office designers are now planning "stand up" meeting rooms because a substantial body of research shows standing shortens meeting length significantly.

In general, there are proven health benefits from standing. Dr. John Buckley and a team of researchers from England's University of Chester conducted a simple experiment. They asked ten people who worked in an office to stand for at least three hours a day for a week. A 2013 BBC report, "Calorie burner: How much better is standing up than sitting?" showed getting to your feet is just plain good for you.

> *The Chester researchers took measurements on days when the volunteers stood, and when they sat around. When they looked at the data there were some striking differences. (Specifically) blood glucose levels fell back to normal levels after a meal far more quickly on the days when the volunteers stood than when they sat. There was also evidence, from the heart rate monitors that they were wearing, that by standing they were burning more calories.*

It only makes sense. If you're standing, you can move around much more easily, and the next thing you know you can skip that extra trip to the gym, right? Okay, maybe not, but it's worthy of some thought.

Read the Room

It's important to read the room, especially if standing is a bit of a stretch in your work culture. If you do stand to speak, perhaps mention you are mixing it up a bit by standing—and not trying to show anyone up. Some in the group may not be comfortable standing, and that's okay, but endless hours (even just one hour) of sitting and presenting can get pretty boring. Standing gives you a chance to move around, keep your audience engaged, and just provides a change of pace.

Ultimately, you'll make that judgment based on the situation, but I hope this chapter helps you at least consider standing to speak at your next meeting.

Where Do I Stand?

If your answer to this question is always, "Right behind the lectern," let's try to expand your horizon a bit. Anytime you stand to speak, you should be aware of your space—move around a bit, give the audience something different to look at. A lectern is fine, but can you also step to the side of it for a time? Can you change things up a bit? And how about not speaking from the stage at all? Often, if a line of speakers has come before me in a meeting, I start at the back of the room or from my seat—just to get people looking somewhere new for a while.

Do you get feedback in your workplace that people

want fewer meetings or they find the meetings boring? I just came from working with a high-profile Silicon Valley firm, and one of the executives I was working with estimated he has thirty meetings a week. When do people have time to think, let alone work? And I'm sure he's not alone. If the volume of the meetings can't be controlled, then how about changing the part you play in those meetings? Or how about mixing up what they look like?

If you are known as a solid speaker who leads better, higher quality meetings, your colleagues will actually want to show up. That can be accomplished, in part, by mixing up where people stand, sit, and how they present to the group. No budget items change, no extreme effort has to be exerted; you can simply change the physical experience of the meeting and make a positive difference in everyone's day.

Use the Tools

If it's a big room that comes equipped with presentation tools, use them. If there's a wireless microphone available, take advantage of it. You don't have to run around the room, but the wireless does give you freedom to move. The same goes for a simple wireless slide advance device. And how about lighting? Is it any wonder people nod off in meetings when we have them sitting in the dark? Or the speaker is lost in shadows? Or the room is so bright the people in the back can't see the screen? Give yourself a better chance of success by thinking through all of these elements.

If you are a featured speaker, always know the room in which you'll present when possible. The more you know about it, the more comfortable you'll be, and the better you'll do when it's your turn to stand up to speak. I always say to clients, "Go to sleep the night before having mentally practiced in the room in which you will be speaking the next day." Very simply, you can process your message in that meeting before it ever happens.

The *Get Great* Point

Stand up, sit down, walk, or don't—at least realize those options exist and think about them. Too often, we think of meetings and speaking in standardized, clichéd terms. No one is suggesting you suddenly turn into David Copperfield. Just bring some imagination and energy to the meeting and speaking process and everyone will appreciate it. Too little effort is being put into the millions of meetings going on every week in our American work culture, and we all suffer when that happens.

WHAT DO I DO ABOUT MY SPEAKING VOICE?

Not all of us are blessed with a voice like James Earl Jones or Catherine Zeta-Jones (not related). In fact, almost none of us can match their unique vocal gifts— that's why voice quality need not be nearly as great a concern as it often is. The point of this chapter is for you to assess and use your voice just as you would any communication tool. It is your instrument and you want to realize it offers you options. It also gives me a chance to tell you a story about someone I ran across who had a voice that could stop you in your tracks. But more on that later.

The Really Good News

When you get up to speak, almost no one is expecting a theatrical production; they just want you to demonstrate your knowledge, perspective, and passion for your topic. Now think of the careers of Lucille Ball, Joe Pesci, and Jim Parsons from *The Big Bang Theory*— none were blessed with great voices, and all were probably told many times they needed to do something about that. But they all still made their mark in the most public forums possible and, in many ways, did it with the help of their unique voices.

So let's say you feel you were not blessed with the best voice possible. Use it! If it is uniquely high, low, scratchy, or squeaky, embrace it. When you speak in a high-stakes situation or in front of people who are hearing you for the first time, address the elephant in the room. Joke about it, acknowledge it, or somehow address it up front and then move on. People will give you credit for your self-knowledge and it will be far less of an issue once it has been addressed.

This is not to say a challenging voice is never a problem. Women, especially, are judged harshly on this issue. Author Audrey Nelson, PhD, wrote about the issue in her 2004 book. In a 2013 *Psychology Today* article, "Work Voice Versus Home Voice: A Women's [sic] Dilemma," Nelson says:

> *Men react negatively to female vocal characteristics that undermine authority: high pitch, slow pace, or increased inflection. British Prime Minister Margaret Thatcher spent hours with a voice tutor doing "humming" exercises to lower the unpleasantly high pitch of her speaking voice.*

Man or woman, if this sounds like you, there is nothing wrong with following Mrs. Thatcher's lead and getting some help. Breathing tricks, making sure you practice, and mixing up the types of talks where colleagues or customers hear you speak (formal and informal) can lessen the impact of a challenging voice. A voice coach can provide specific suggestions, such as remembering to speak from your diaphragm instead of your nose if you have a high, squeaky voice. Also, if you tend to lose your breath, practice making a single point with each sentence, and watch the punctuation. (Most "breathy" speakers run right through the natural stop signs that can help them slow down.) If you have a unique, quirky voice, you can hope the audience will remember your message because of the way you acknowledged what otherwise might have been considered a flaw.

Bottom line, have an accurate picture of your situation. We can be overly self-conscious about things like the sound of our voice, so only address it if you've been told several times people are surprised or distracted by the unique quality of your voice. Otherwise, forget about it. You may feel your voice is distracting or different, but if others don't notice it, move on.

Think of it this way: your voice is an extension of your personality. Just as what you wear and the way you walk help make you who you are, so your voice helps define you. Embrace it. Understand it. Play off of it if you can. Use it as a tool to help get your point across.

For many years, one of the most highly paid business speakers in the country has been former college football coach Lou Holtz. Lou is generally older than his audience and has a raspy, high voice, some speech challenges, and big ears. He's also one of the best, most engaging—not to mention most memorable—speakers out there because he uses *all* of those items to his advantage.

A Memorable "Hello"

Finally, that story about one of the best voices I ever had the pleasure to hear. One of my fondest memories from my years working in Hollywood was the day I crossed paths with singer Lou Rawls. On the day I met him, he was walking toward me on the Paramount Studios lot. I said, "Hi."

He smiled and responded, "Hey, how are you doing?"

Just like that, you knew he had the kind of voice that was unmistakable. It could actually stop you. Hearing Lou Rawls, with that deep baritone instrument, is something very few people could forget. He truly had a great, unique voice. Check out his videos online—it's worth it.

The *Get Great* Point

Have a realistic view of your voice and take measures, if necessary. Just like any characteristic, we can be distracted and held back by it or we can get help and realize the opportunity it provides. We can be worried about the things we don't like about ourselves or we can work to change it. Chances are, someone else in the audience also feels the same way about themselves. Provide a great, positive example for them, and you'll do more good than you might ever know.

HELP! I HAVE A PRESENTATION AND NO PREP TIME!

Does this sound like you? The boss says you need to speak tomorrow, and you're totally booked between now and then. Or a team member can't be there and you suddenly have to fill in for them. Or you've said you can be the go-to person at work, but you've already over-committed on other things. Whatever the situation, you probably know the feeling: *How can I ever get this right if I don't have time to prepare?*

With all of the consolidations that occurred after the post-2008 recession, many workplaces are experiencing exactly what I just described. Doing more with less became a worldwide mantra, and something we all need to realize is that this is the new normal. Does it sometimes seem overwhelming? You bet. Are you alone? Not a chance. The answer is to be as smart as possible in managing your time and know when to say no. My goal is to give you tools to help manage any surprise speaking situation you might face.

Keep It Simple

I recently visited one of my favorite places—the Lincoln Memorial in Washington, DC. The Gettysburg Address is on one wall, and whenever I read it, I'm blown away by the succinct clarity of that extremely powerful speech. President Lincoln knew the importance of keeping it simple. A short timeframe with limited prep time gives you an opportunity to practice exactly that: keeping it simple. And who doesn't love it when a speech, meeting, or presentation is done early? Instead of burying yourself with an unreasonable amount of material, pare the presentation down to **the three biggest points** that have to be made and start from there.

In Fact, Start Right Now!

Just take five minutes and a 3 × 5 index card and jot down a few notes on the major points you might need to explain the work you do or the current project for which you are responsible. Keep it in your purse or jacket pocket over the next twenty-four hours, and don't expand it to a big legal pad or electronic device. What you're doing is giving yourself a start on that surprise presentation. It may not occur for a month or two, but when the call does come you'll already have started a roadmap for what otherwise might seem overwhelming.

Sleep On It

Harvard Medical School research, outlined in the *Harvard Gazette* article "Learning While We Sleep and Dream," shows if we can turn ideas over in our heads while we sleep, the finished product can come out with more clarity. Jeffrey Ellenbogen, who helped lead the Harvard research, says, "Our results strongly imply that sleep is actively engaged in the cognitive processing of our memories. Knowledge appears to expand both over time and with sleep."

No time to prep? Let your brain work on this one while you sleep.

Use PowerPoint to Cheat

This is a two-step process. Assemble a simple PowerPoint presentation based on your 3 × 5 card notes. Use the PowerPoint to remind yourself what you are talking about when you stand up to speak with no preparation. Don't read the slides word for word; just use them to jog your memory. You can easily speak on short notice with little warning when you've already assembled the foundational items of your latest project or work assignment.

Other Quick Suggestions:

1. Make it a "team" presentation. Turn it into an interview instead of a speech by providing expert Q&A.

2. Take the basics of one of your earlier talks and tweak it.

Don't Get Distracted by the Negatives

If you've been thinking during this chapter, *Well, that won't work for me because . . .* , please stop! Sure, there are always things that keep any solution from being the *perfect* solution. If you only think about the way a suggestion doesn't fit, you'll struggle to make any kind of progress.

The *Get Great* Point

We are all being asked to do more in less time; use these tips to help solve the dilemma. Remember, many people are a little wigged out about giving a speech—your audience will understand your situation (and have probably faced it many times themselves) when you are working on a quick deadline. If appropriate, you can even mention you just learned you were speaking yesterday, and instead of making it a negative, say you're glad to have this opportunity. You get points for your professionalism and can make your situation relatable, because, these days, everyone has been there—including me.

In 2005, NBC news anchor Brian Williams was scheduled to emcee a national conference dinner but was called away to the Katrina floods in New Orleans and had to cancel. I was asked to fill in. The whole audience was expecting to see Williams in a tuxedo at the lectern, and I knew it. Rather than ignore the obvious, I addressed it early on: "Many of you were expecting to see Brian Williams here tonight. To say I was a last-minute replacement would be an understatement. A few minutes ago I was out parking cars in the valet line. Luckily I was dressed for the part."

PART FOUR:

THE SIMPLE, OVERLOOKED SKILLS

SAY WHAT?

Why Listening Needs to Be Taught in Every School on the Planet

"My name is Donald. Like Donald Duck." And with that, I never forgot his name. It might sound silly, but how else do you get someone to remember your name? One common lament I hear is the struggle people have remembering names. Knowing this, you can help others out by doing something to get them to remember yours. (With people of a certain age I often say, when introducing myself, "I'm Cary. Like Cary Grant." It doesn't work for everyone, but you get the idea.)

All of this is tied to the idea of **listening**. Not hearing, but really listening. The guy named Donald is one of the best customer service experts I've ever met. What's his secret? Besides his history of working undercover for the FBI (more on that later), he's an excellent listener. If you want to **Get Great,** you'll have to improve your listening skills.

Are You Trained?

Think about the training you've received in your life. If you ever studied communication, your schooling included classes for reading and writing, and maybe you took a speech class. As an adult, perhaps you've been trained in a sales seminar or customer-service workshop. Have you ever attended a class called "Listening 101"?

Listening is one of the most important skills we can develop; yet we do nothing to help people on this front. Amazing. It really is a talent that needs to be nurtured and taught in every school and workplace on the planet. So, let's take a small first step right now!

First, understand that listening is actually a pretty difficult skill to master. Know why? One reason is our brains work faster than our mouths. Simply put, while someone else is talking, we are often ahead of them—our brain is moving at three times the speed of the words the other person is putting out. The average person speaks at about 125 words per minute. The average listener can comprehend information much more quickly, so listeners' minds tend to wander—and the next thing you know your audience hasn't heard a word you've said for the last thirty or forty seconds. While you've been talking, they've been off thinking about other issues or taking your line of reasoning in a completely different direction.

The clever storyteller will sometimes play on exactly that tendency. They know enough about the human condition and how we are wired to use it against us. Have you ever listened to a story and started to come to your own conclusion, only to have the storyteller slam that door shut, knowing that's exactly where your brain was going? We are often predictably distracted when we listen to others.

Writer and counselor Dianne Schilling writes on Forbes.com, "10 Steps to Effective Listening" in November of 2012, about the true value of listening, especially today. "Genuine listening has become a rare gift—the gift of time. It helps build relationships, solve problems, ensure understanding, resolve conflicts, and improve accuracy."

Sound and communication expert Julian Treasure says, "We're losing our listening," in one of his TED Talks from July of 2011 entitled "5 Ways to Listen Better." Treasure notes modern tools and distractions—from constant noises to our ever-present headphones to the simple fact almost anything can be recorded—that devalue listening. Why listen when you can simply get a recording of it and listen later? (Which often means never.)

There are two very important issues to remember when you think about listening. First, what listening means for you as a speaker. Second, what listening means for you as a listener, employee, team player, or audience member.

As a Speaker: If you know your audience may wander off at any given moment, it brings a certain urgency to your message. You realize that the ten minutes of history and detail you had planned for the presentation may need to be shortened and made more relevant to the audience.

While detail and background are important, you have to realize you can also lose people when they feel the information has little connection to their lives. While you're speaking at 125 words a minute, your audience is trying to find an idea they can jump on—but not for long. Suddenly they're thinking about what they need to pick up at the store on the drive home.

Perhaps you've been accused of being a "sentence finisher?" You keep finishing other people's sentences before they get the words out. (Tried and convicted!) It is not only an annoying habit, but also proof the listeners are often trying to jump ahead.

As a Listener: While not all of us are giving presentations every day, we are all listening—whether at home, on the job, or just out in everyday life. Listening skills can be THE KEY to how people judge your leadership abilities, especially if you're in management.

A good listener grasps IDEAS, not just facts. While the individual facts are important, piecing together the IDEAS and listening for all of the cues the speaker is providing results in far better listening and better overall communication.

Practice **active listening**. Pay special attention to what a person is saying, and then offer a summary of what you understand is being said when you're in one-on-one conversation or small groups. And it's not just about the feedback; in the same TED Talk, Julian

Treasure refers to the way you sit or stand while all of this is happening, referring to "listening positions." He says, "You can move your listening position to what's appropriate to what you're listening to." In active listening, we need to not only be listening and reflecting on what we're hearing, but we need to LOOK like we're listening as well.

Now back to Donald—as in Donald Duck—whom I mentioned at the beginning of this chapter. Don simply stands out as soon as you meet him. Have you ever met someone like this? Those people who just seem sharper, more with it, more present and attentive? They are hard not to like because they're paying more attention. They're taking the extra step to understand who you are. Simply put, they are good listeners.

In Don's case, I just had to know his backstory—and it's worth knowing. When he was a young man, his buddies dared him to respond to a newspaper ad from the FBI. As a Bay-area skateboarding kid, he didn't exactly fit the image of the no-nonsense FBI culture—and that's exactly why the FBI hired him. Don wasn't hired as an agent but as a staffer who also ended up doing undercover work. He didn't fit the profile. He could slip into certain worlds where an average gun-carrying agent could not.

As you might imagine, working undercover for the FBI demands that you keep your listening skills sharp because you're likely to be called upon to write detailed reports or testify in high-profile criminal cases. Oh, and people may want to kill you for what you recall, so it's always best to remember correctly!

In a strange twist of fate, a hack of security records ended up making his identity public and Don had to cut short his undercover career. At the same time, family needs resulted in his moving to a completely different area of the country and starting a new career. These days, Don can be found helping run a luxury automobile dealership. Guess what? His listening skills still come in handy. What are your expectations walking into a luxury car dealership? Definitely something extra, and Don is the perfect person to deliver on that expectation.

The *Get Great* Point

Better listening results in less busywork and fewer meetings, and eliminates the need for endless reminder memos. Leaders who understand what's actually happening in the listening process (*Hey, the audience's minds will tend to wander!*) speak with fewer asides and more focus. They also summarize effectively, rewarding those who have listened well and bringing clarity to those who may have gotten lost along the way. They are often more respected by employees because of their listening skill. Everyone who practices effective listening needs fewer follow-up meetings, emails, and babysitting.

Good listeners make better bosses and effective employees. This book is not intended as a how-to on listening, but if you come away valuing the skill of listening, you are likely to be much more successful as a communicator. (If you search out a listening class and find it works, let me know about it.)

"YOU TALKIN' TO ME?"

Eye Contact and Finding the Right Balance

Every successful person I can think of understands the importance of eye contact. They might not all be good at it, but they value it. There was one senior executive I worked with who, I noticed, had the nervous habit of looking around the room while having a conversation. Nobody engaging in conversation wants the sensation that they are about to be supplanted by someone more important who just happens to walk into view. Such are the perils of flaky eye contact and the weight it carries, often unknowingly, for all of us.

The right balance that I mentioned in the subtitle is a great starting point. Many times when we are trying to work on something, we feel self-conscious about it—which can be evident in our level of eye contact and what we do with our eyes. Shifty eyes and staring without blinking are two noticeable signs of nervousness.

The words that inspired this chapter came from a menacing line delivered by Robert De Niro's character in the movie *Taxi Driver*: "Are you talkin' to me?" The frightening stare that complements the line—never breaking contact—is the scary, evil relative in the eye contact family. While staying connected to the people you are in conversation with is important, too much of a good thing is definitely *not* a good thing. Words like "creepy," "weird," and "odd" should never be associated with you if you want to gain the trust of others, and a practice of staring inappropriately could earn those titles very quickly.

Measuring How Much This Matters

Now that we've addressed that whole staring thing (and I have one more important thought about it a little later), let's explore just how much our lives are driven by eye contact. There is a ton of research on the topic, but one of the most interesting pieces of work was recently done by Cornell researcher Brian Wansink as seen in the *Environment & Behavior* article, "Eyes in the Aisles: Why is Cap'n Crunch Looking Down at My Child?" The research shows how much we actually search out eye contact because we have such a strong need for it. Wansink and his fellow researchers studied products that feature cartoon characters and found that cereals aimed at kids, for example, actually had the eyes of the cartoon characters cast down so as to be looking right at their young consumers. When the Trix rabbit did not look directly at the consumer, sales dropped. Check out how many products actually stare at you from the shelves of your local grocery store. It's not by accident—we want to look and be looked at.

A new parent will stare lovingly into the eyes of a new baby for hours. Why? It's more than just fascination with new creation—it is vitally important to that child's development. Babies who get that kind of attention, research from the National Center for Infants, Toddlers and Families shows, have a better chance of growing into well-adjusted adults. On the flip side, infants who are denied healthy attention often have difficulty developing a healthy brain. We're wired to crave eye contact; denial of that desire can have serious implications.

Now think about the impact of all of the devices with which you interact—what happens to eye contact when you are constantly checking your phone during a conversation with an employee, spouse, friend, or child? Children will sit at a family meal at a restaurant and spend the entire time watching a screen. I understand parents sometimes need a break, but how did families from earlier generations handle this situation? And what impact will this device-happy world have on the development of long-term connectivity skills like empathy, friendship, and our overall ability to listen to one another?

In an excellent piece by Kate Murphy in the *New York Times,* "Psst. Look Over Here," on May 16, 2014, Murphy summarizes the importance of looking up from that tablet, laptop, or phone:

Only actual eye contact fully activates those parts of the brain that allow us to more acutely and accurately process another person's feelings and intentions. Think of it as a cognitive jump-start that occurs whenever you lock eyes with another person, whether in front of you or across a crowded room.

Even the brains of legally blind people have been shown to light up when someone looks them in the eye. It's a sort of primal awareness and why you sometimes feel someone is looking at you before you turn and see them.

It's a fascinating topic, and it's pretty darn important. So how do you make sure you are headed in the right direction with your eye contact?

You Can't Do This Alone

Trying to correctly measure how you are doing with eye contact—not to mention assuming you can measure it on your own—is a mistake. It takes another pair of eyes.

Have others already told you eye contact isn't your strong point? Do you sense you could be better? Do you think technology is getting in your way? Any or all of these can be an issue, and the best way to get a read on it is to ask. Before you commit to working with a professional to improve (which could be a great idea if you're really struggling), ask those around you: "Do you feel I look at you when we are talking?" "How is my eye contact?" and "Do I ever stare?"

Or perhaps the issue can be framed more generally, without focusing on eye contact directly: "How do I do in meetings—do I connect with the team?" "Do you think people 'get' me?" "How can I get clients to feel more of a connection to me?"

People you can count on will speak honestly with you, especially if you have a history of asking for real, honest feedback and direction from others. If you make a habit of having these conversations and take them seriously, you'll build a reputation of leadership and maturity, no matter what your official job title says.

In Conversation

Position your body so eye contact comes easily and seems as natural as possible. Sitting across from someone, or together comfortably in a group, is the simplest and most important baseline in fostering great eye contact. Come out from behind a desk, step a bit closer (but not too close), and look them in the eye. Again, balance is important, but make a conscious effort to connect with the eyes of others as you speak with them, checking in every sentence or two with a direct look.

Gazing off as you gather your thoughts is not an issue, but staring off as you speak for more than thirty seconds or so can create a disconnect. Remember, your conversation partner's brain is moving three times faster than you can speak—it will wander unless you keep your conversation partner engaged. One of the best ways to keep someone engaged is to maintain eye contact.

During a Speech

Much has been written about how you should "work the room" with your eye contact during a speech. My advice is far less structured than most. Instead of instituting a "look at an audience member for five seconds and then move to another" rule, I instead ask that you spread your eye contact around in a way that makes sense for your message. Make sure you are either connecting with individuals—or sections of the audience if you have a bigger crowd—on a regular basis. Most speakers show a right or left side preference unknowingly. Do you? Watch the video or ask someone to pay attention and provide you with feedback. If you seem to favor one side over the other, see if you can fix it. No one in your audience wants to feel they are being overlooked.

Even in large rooms, try to connect with individuals. It's a great way of saying, *Sure, this is a big crowd, but each of you matters to me.* I've seen many experienced speakers gaze over the top of the crowd—big mistake. Even when the audience is in the dark, act like you are looking at individuals. You may not be able to see them specifically, but the effect will be as if you are looking directly at different people, and the audience will appreciate it.

The *Get Great* Point

Isn't it telling that even in a large crowd we want to be seen? We want to feel connected with the person at the front. Great speakers make this connection a priority, and it's often one of the reasons they are viewed as great speakers. So if it's important in a room of a thousand people, you know it's **critical** in a room with two. Make it a priority to put down the phone. Respect everyone with whom you are having an important conversation. Your effort will be appreciated and you will **stand out** by focusing on one of the most fundamental elements of communication.

CASTING YOUR NEXT PRESENTATION

How to Incorporate Casting Daily (and How My Daughter Got on *American Idol*)

My daughter Katie can sing and dance and, of course, I think she's really talented; but she wasn't actually a contestant on *American Idol*. (Yes, another story about one of my kids.) Here's the weird thing: she was still there, sitting right by Jennifer Lopez. How did that come to be? Well, it is all about casting—and casting is used far more often than you might realize. The more you know about it, the more you may realize you should be using it in your business decisions.

So here's the story—and how it can relate to your next presentation.

Katie was on spring break during her first year at college and found a vacation option that fit her limited budget. She went to Los Angeles, and she was cast as an audience member for the taping of a TV show. At first she didn't even know which show she would be seeing, but she got to see some fun stuff and actually made a little money along the way. You see, when filming TV shows, the producers specifically select the people who are within camera view. Katie had gone to a website that recruited audience members—and here's the key—they asked for her picture.

Is it any surprise that an attractive young woman (she gets her looks from her mom) would end up sitting right behind the most telegenic judge on the program? That night, there she was—big as life on national TV. Sure, no big recording contract, but a fun spring break memory for her.

How Do You Cast Your Meetings And Presentations?

Most leaders make decisions about who plays an "out front" role based on skillset or knowledge of the material. Not bad, but let's consider some other factors. What will the audience respond to? What are key influences for the decision makers? Who has shown potential and would *not* be one of the usual suspects? What are the priorities of the group, company, or client? Does your team reflect those priorities?

Guess what? You need to be a casting director, and you didn't even know it.

This means you have to start developing your talent early because you never know when you might have to cast someone in a new or expanded role down the road. Your team will appreciate that you're looking out for their future opportunities, and your bosses will appreciate that you have more than just three people who can take on new responsibilities. Everybody wins.

How Do You Find Those Future Stars?

Many times, an outsider can give you more perspective on this topic than you can gain after months or even years of interacting with the same people. Need to spot an overlooked gem? Have a colleague from a different office or division spend some time with your team. Get a consultant in to do some training and see what he or she notices. A new pair of eyes can provide fresh insight. And finally, what does the team think? Maybe they will offer up a surprise addition to the presentation group (whom you would have overlooked), which then injects new energy to the entire process. Remember, this new cast member doesn't have to be the star of the show; he or she may play a small part, but you can start building his or her confidence for future roles down the road.

Finding the Hidden Treasures

Sir Ken Robinson is famous for his TED talks and writings on discovering your talents. As a leader—with a title or not—you are well served by being on a constant search for talent. Robinson describes this in his talk "Bring on the Learning Revolution!": "Human resources are like the earth's natural resources: they're often buried deep. You have to go looking for them, they're not just lying around on the surface."

The extra time you spend realizing that the otherwise-quiet colleague is actually the most strategic thinker in the room (the quiet ones often are) is a huge step forward for both of you. Not only have you improved the capability of the entire room, you've helped that person understand the role he or she can play, and you are now viewed as an effective leader. Yes, you are a casting director.

What If You're Not the Boss?

You don't have to wait around for someone else to make this point, by the way. The bosses don't always have all the best ideas. But your suggestion of different cast members for a meeting shouldn't come out of the blue; the best way to be heard is to set the groundwork in place over time. If you provide helpful suggestions and positive feedback for your fellow employees and are seen as a skilled strategist, your suggestion of mixing up the usual suspects will have a chance to be welcomed.

What about when your team has been fighting an uphill battle to get attention, jobs, or new business? A new cast may be exactly what will help bring about a breakthrough. No matter if you're the boss or one of the newer team members, think about mixing things up a bit in hopes of creating a different outcome.

The *Get Great* Point

Show business pros make everything look so effortless because they use the same rules as every other successful business. They put in the hard work, and they pay attention to detail. So, take a page out of the Hollywood producers' handbook: Cast your presentations well and keep an eye to your audience. Develop your talent knowing you'll have to call upon a variety of people along the way. While it takes some extra effort, in the end it will reflect well on you as well as your team. And the next time you're watching a TV show, remember: it isn't just the name performers who are purposely cast.

HUMOR

Why Only Two Kinds of Jokes Actually Work

Sitting backstage at the Hermosa Beach Comedy and Magic Club, you can see history all around you. My friend Jimmy Burns lives in the area and from time to time he'll bring me along as he drops by to see friends and fellow comedians. The room is regularly inhabited by the very best in the stand-up world: Jerry Seinfeld, Arsenio Hall, Jay Leno, and all the others. They have all been here many times, and they are a fascinating group. Quick, wickedly observant, and sometimes merciless in their commentary, this is not a group to hang out with if you are the sensitive type. That being said, many comedians also call upon a deep-seated sensitivity to bring their humor—and sometimes their pain—to the surface in front of a room full of strangers. This is one of the most valuable insights we can garner from comedians: how to gauge our audience, and how to do it quickly.

If you have coworkers who always want to start

their talk with a joke, notice how many times it actually works. And does it work with everyone? Really take a mental survey of the room. How many genuine future–Jimmy Fallons are out there?

If you look through the stacks of books on public speaking at your local bookstore, you'll often see, nearby, the latest joke books. The logic on this is simple: anyone who has to appear in front of an audience will surely want to liven up their presentation with a joke or two—or ten. As appealing as that may sound, use extreme caution. In fact, my advice is to step back from the jokes! Now, that doesn't mean you should never try to get a laugh out of your audience, but there is a much better middle ground, and there are really two, **and only two**, kinds of jokes that work. First, though, a few words about the rules of the road before you even consider using comedy.

Stay Away from the Obvious

Almost everyone who starts a sentence with, "I want to tell you a joke..." already has two strikes against them and a hard slider coming in. If you take this approach, you will sound like someone straight out of vaudeville, and believe me, vaudeville is dead. Never telegraph that you're about to tell a joke; your audience will immediately think, *Boy, this better be good!* Announcing that you're about to tell a joke is too formal when the end result you're shooting for is laughter.

The next key to good comedy I've learned from the professionals is the importance of **keeping it subtle**. Whacking someone over the head with a joke, any joke, will kill about 80 percent of the humor (we've all heard the person who starts laughing before they get to the punch line). When you deliver a funny line, you're offering up a delicate creation. Don't be careless about how it's handled. When I think of the biggest laughs I've gotten from audiences, the common thread is that the audience had no idea the joke was coming.

It's also important to spend time perfecting your *overall* speech, because there is a chance that the joke won't hit home for everyone. Too often we become so downhearted when a joke doesn't work, especially at the beginning of the speech, we lose energy and focus for the rest of the presentation. The purpose of the speech isn't to make the audience laugh; it can still be effective even if it isn't funny.

So, you've heard what *not* to do. Here are the two things you *should* do if you're going to incorporate humor:

The Two Kinds of Jokes That Work

IF—and this is a big if—you are going to make fun of anyone, make sure it is one and only one person.

You.

Self-deprecating humor works because when you poke fun at yourself, you get the laugh *and* the relief from the audience when they realize you're not making fun of them or something they care about. Think about the opposite option. Making fun of anything or anyone else nearly guarantees someone—and maybe a large chunk of the audience—won't think it is funny and may be totally ticked off.

If you've ever seen or attended a "roast," you know what I'm talking about. In an attempt to skewer the guest of honor, the harpoon is shot off course, and the audience is squirming uncomfortably—or booing loudly. To assume we know the mindset of every person in the audience is foolhardy at best—you can never know everyone's history, beliefs, preferences, and values. All of those, and many others, are factors in the mental checklist we carry around when we are deciding whether or not something is funny. And even if you know a joke would hit home with a colleague one-on-one, he or she may not laugh in a room full of other people; just like I might laugh at one kind of joke with my college students but not with a senior-citizens group.

In 1980, when Reagan was the Republican nominee for president, the biggest obstacle he faced was his age. At sixty-eight, Reagan looked noticeably older than President Jimmy Carter, and some said he was just too old to be president, especially considering he would be (and was) nearly eighty when he finished two four-year terms in office.

Knowing this, and being a master at understanding the mindset of an audience after years in Hollywood,

Reagan would say the following to a serious-minded but sometimes skeptical audience: "The great leaders of our country, Washington, Jefferson, Benjamin Franklin, Lincoln . . ." And then, after a suitable pause: "I knew many of these men . . ."

By making himself the butt of the joke, he also addressed the elephant in the room without being on the defensive. Laughter can truly be great medicine, but you want to be careful and smart in how you dispense it.

For the other form of humor that works, your powers of observation will serve you well.

Situational humor is a trickier option, but has even more of a potential upside. This is rarely a joke you work on ahead of time (the tricky part) because it plays off of what has already happened in the room that day. The reason this can still be a safe option is that you have already gotten a chance to take the temperature of the room. You've witnessed the way your audience reacted to the situation and you can be pretty sure you know their mindset.

Caution still has to be exercised, though, because even moment to moment, the comedic temperature in the room can change. But generally, a situational joke demonstrates you're paying attention, and the bigger laugh is the result of the shared knowledge on the origins of the joke.

To explain, here's a simple situation that wraps all of this comedy theory together: While spending a few hours with a group in a workshop setting, I had stumbled and misremembered a detail about one of the well-liked people in the group, Amber. Feeling a bit embarrassed, I filed it away. About thirty minutes later, when another glitch came up with the AV equipment in the room and I was having a bit of a struggle, I said, "This time I'm just going to have Amber come up and save me because things are clearly getting way out of hand." **The joke was self-deprecating AND situational.**

The audience appreciates when you remember one of their favorite people—as Amber was—and I wasn't making fun of anyone but myself.

The *Get Great* Point

Work at this stuff! Don't just buy a joke book and read off a few choice items. If you want to use humor, work on material that will really mean something to your audience. Humor is most successful when it's been thought out. Sure, we love it when the lucky accident happens and everyone enjoys the moment, but an even better situation for an experienced presenter is when a big laugh happens because it *looks like* a lucky accident!

AN EASY WAY TO KEEP GETTING GREAT

Why Serious Practice Holds the Key

Hopefully, you have found value in this book (and the fact that you are reading these words indicates that you have); one of my final points is to provide you with a tool to keep this process moving.

What if you could keep **Getting Great** at the communication process all the time? I believe you can, and it doesn't even require that much effort.

Do You Practice? How?

Who has time to practice? While many of us understand the VALUE of practicing for an important interview, presentation, or conversation, we often end up winging it anyway; or we relive college and pull an all-nighter before that important meeting (only making it worse) to prepare those last-minute details. My goal here is to give you some tips that help make those precious practice sessions—because you do need them—as productive as possible.

Make it real: Too often, practice is just **play**. Your discussion within your team, for example, will go something like this: *"You do that, then I'll say this, and then we'll end this way, okay?"* But not taking practice seriously is one of the best ways to sink a big opportunity. Make your practice as realistic as possible. Do it in a room similar to the one you will face on the big day, and run through it UNINTERRUPTED. If you are stopping and making changes all the time, you never have a true feel for what the final product will actually look like. Early practices might be a little rough, but as you get closer to the event, you need to make the session as real as possible.

Use a camera: Yes, I know people hate it and I've said it before, but a camera is the very best teaching tool. You can talk about Bob's lack of charisma, but when Bob sees himself on camera he suddenly realizes he needs to pump up the energy! The camera forces you to listen to your voice and see your gestures (or lack of them) and saves you a lot of time in fine-tuning the finished product. Going to a job interview? Pull out your phone and record yourself telling your story. It will help tremendously.

Get an outsider's opinion: Whether you hire a professional coach or ask Maria down the hall to come in for some feedback, get an outsider's opinion. Many times you're just too close to the material to be able to offer a true, fresh outlook on the overall message. As you get closer to the finish line, make sure someone from the outside sees how you are doing.

Ask for specific feedback from your team: How many times have you done a run-through of a major project, and when you ask for feedback you hear, "It was fine." "Good." "Okay." None of those comments tell you anything! **Ask for specific feedback ahead of time.** Let your colleagues know you are working on this weak spot or trying to improve this strength and you need to know if it's working. Being specific is the only way you can know if you are getting better. Direct the feedback and the team will start pulling in the same direction, working on each individual's goals.

Practice time is extremely important. The most successful communicators I know would not go in front of a camera or an audience without **serious practice**. Adopt that same policy starting today. Take practice seriously and you will be on the road to constant improvement.

The *Get Great* Point

Let me help you on this journey. Sign up for my **Monthly Memo** and receive fresh advice on these critical topics the last week of every month. Follow me on Twitter, @CaryPfeffer, for links to helpful articles (and some fun observations on life around us). My goal is to be a resource to you and my website, NoAppBook.com, will be a place to continue the conversation. Finally, let me know how you are applying these thoughts and observations. Thank you so very much for spending some of your time reading this book.

Now, my last piece of advice for you . . .

SMILE: IT'S THAT SIMPLE

If you remember NOTHING else from this book, remember the title of this chapter.

Seriously.

The simplest piece of advice I can provide for you is that a smile will do more for you than just about anything else in this book.

So why have I waited this long to tell you? Because context is important. If you selected the book and saw this advice on the first page, you might think you made a mistake. *Too simple*, you'd think. But is it? Everything we've talked about up until now sets the groundwork for this important notion. If you understand something about body language, gestures, and the power of first impressions, then you are more likely to appropriately value a smile.

And here's why you've paid good money to have someone tell you to smile. Because, often, we *have* to be told! I have worked with literally thousands of smart, accomplished people. Almost across the board, I've had to remind them to smile.

Why We Struggle with the Smile

The first step in understanding why we rarely smile when we really should is to think about when we *naturally* smile. We smile when we're happy. When we are around people we like. When we are RELAXED! Now think about having a critical conversation, giving a speech, or going into a job interview or a room full of strangers. Smiling now?

My guess is that you're not.

The moment when we are hoping to come across well, connect with someone, or make a good first impression, we tend to tense up, we close down, we put on—at the very least—a passive face, and more often we look like we're ticked off!

The RBF Phenomenon

If you don't know about RBF, don't worry (I may act like I'm a smarty pants, but one of my daughters had to tell me what RBF means). RBF stands for "Resting Bitch Face."

Have you seen it? Do you have one? We don't always know it, but we can carry around a very unfriendly, serious face. And it can turn people off from twenty feet away. Usually, someone has to tell us we are suffering from the RBF phenomenon; we might be scowling and we don't even know it. It happens all the time.

In practice sessions with many a CEO—prepping

them for big, often exciting announcements—I've used a camera to capture the initial run-through. And, without fail, these clients look as if they're heading to a funeral while saying things like, "This is an exciting day for the Acme Company and all of our team members . . ."

I play the video back for them, and they are shocked by what they see. Then I ask them why they think they have that look on their face. The usual response? "Well, this is a big deal. It's a major step for our company. I'm really concerned and I want everything to go just right."

My response? "Well, a great first step would be for you to smile a little when you say these words." And with that we are headed in the right direction.

Try This

When I started this chapter, I actually stopped writing for about a week and conducted a very unscientific—but quite telling—experiment. I purposely went out and smiled at people. I know that might sound weird, but stick with me for a second. If you want to see the effect smiling can have, give this a try. Walking down the street? Have a simple, friendly look on your face. On a crowded airplane? Greet strangers with a smile. In a room with a mix of people you know and others you don't? Make a concerted effort to offer a genuine smile.

See what happens.

I'm willing to bet you'll get one of two reactions: the people you encounter will either return the favor, or they'll be completely surprised—it doesn't often happen that a stranger offers a genuine smile, and it can throw people off for a second. (I almost preferred that reaction—I had shaken their day, and we never even exchanged a word!) The key to the experiment is to go about your day as usual, changing only the expression you have on your face.

Yale University professor and author Marianne LaFrance has done noteworthy research on this topic. She cites studies in a Yale Scientific article called "Subtle Smile," demonstrating people who have physical or mental limitations that make smiling difficult or impossible also have trouble sustaining meaningful relationships. "We need to connect, belong, and have relationships," concludes LaFrance, "and smiling helps us achieve this."

What About Your Yearbook Picture?

How's this for linking your smile with your life: Dacher Keltner of the University of California Berkeley spent thirty years following up on students who displayed wide, confident smiles in their yearbook photos; his research showed those smile-friendly people ended up scoring higher on standardized happiness tests, enjoyed longer, happier marriages, and were viewed as a positive influence on those around them. Better get out that yearbook.

There are cultural, religious, sexual, generational, financial, and political divisions within all of our worlds, and we can certainly see those divides in business. Smiling can bridge them all. The smile says so much beyond the obvious friendly first impression; when you smile, you're saying you are aware of the other person. You're saying you are willing to listen to what they might have to say. You're saying you are open to them, that you are accepting. The smile opens doors.

So What Kind of a Smile are We Talking About?

This actually may require more thought than you would expect. I always point out to clients this is not about having a big, over-the-top 1970s game show–host smile. It has to be genuine and appropriate. It has to demonstrate a level of connection. The researchers call it a Duchenne smile, and you should be smiling with your eyes as well as your mouth. Bottom line? There has to be something behind the smile. And it really is the first step in putting yourself out there—it's the way you begin to demonstrate your value (you still have to be ready to back it up).

Who thought there could be so much behind a simple smile?

Here's why it makes such a difference: When someone has a great, appropriate smile we are much more likely to listen to them, trust them, and invest some of our time in them. We are willing to open up. We'll give someone the benefit of the doubt because he or she seems like a genuine person. Conversely, the frown creates concerns. It raises questions in people's minds: *Is there a problem? Have I unknowingly done something to displease this person? What's wrong?*

The next time you are prepping for an important meeting, speech, or presentation, have all of your thoughts, research, and plans for any objections in order. Then, finally, remind yourself to relax just a bit—and smile.

The *Get Great* Point

When you first meet people, what is the quickest way for them to connect with you? Sure, it's great if you're having a great day, are at the top of your game, or are surrounded by friends. It's helpful to be in a setting that presents you in a positive light, but we don't always have those advantages under our control. Just know that you always have something you can do to stand out and give yourself the best chance of standing out in the crowd.

David Letterman was finishing up his run at the Ed Sullivan Theater in New York City. People were lining up to see the show and every taping was sold out, but I knew that there could be some last-minute open seats on occasion. I walked by an hour or two before the taping time and asked if there might be an extra single seat. I was taken to the production assistant who was handling seating, and I specifically remember thinking to myself, *Smile at this person to let her know you appreciate her effort.* She took my cell number and called within an hour. An open seat had been found. What do you think my chances would have been had I gone with an attitude or assumed the worst? It was certainly not the only factor, but I'm convinced a smile often helps and did in this case.

This is especially important for those who don't see a lot of smiles. Police officers, airline ticket agents, and cell phone store employees come to mind. Do you need something from them? Yeah, so does everyone else. Make their job a little easier by offering an expression of kindness.

Smile. It's that simple.

ACKNOWLEDGMENTS

Writing this book has been a joy, an adventure, and something that wouldn't have been possible without the support, feedback, and love of many people. You know who you are, but it's important to recognize you here.

To my clients: Thank you so much for putting your faith in me and allowing me to learn from you. This book would not be possible without you.

To my Mountain Valley Church family: Thanks for helping me think about what's really important.

To Sweetwood Creative and Pat Hazell for help with the title.

To the students at Arizona State University's W.P. Carey School of Business, who provided the original inspiration for this effort.

To Marquette University High School. You built on what my parents started, and I am forever grateful. Special thanks to Frank.

To Gompers Habilitation Center. A portion of the proceeds from the sale of this book are being donated to Gompers because the important work at Gompers must continue.

Thank you Gregory, Alden, and Heidi for being some of the first to give me feedback and inspiration along the way. To Cassidy and Katie, Kim and Dale, Tami, Neda and Cortney, Jimmy, Pat and John, Troy, Julie, Jeff, Brian, Rick and Rich, Brian and his Y Scouts' energy, Chad, my brother Craig, and everyone else who joined in this journey.

To my kids, who have provided me with endless inspiration: your love and example keeps me going every day.

Finally, to the greatest possible addition to my life—Camille.

BIBLIOGRAPHY

BBC. 2013. "Calorie burner: How much better is standing up than sitting?" *BBC News,* October 16. bbc.com/news/magazine-24532996.

Berkun, Scott. 2010. *Confessions of a Public Speaker.* Sebastopol, ON: O'Reilly Media, Inc.

Blakeslee, Sandra. 2012. "Mind Games: Sometimes a White Coat Isn't Just a White Coat." *The New York Times,* April 22. http://www.nytimes.com/2012/04/03/science/clothes-and-self-perception.html?_r=0.

Casriel, Erika. 2007. "Confidence: Stepping Out." *Psychology Today,* March 1. psychologytoday.com/articles/200702/confidence-stepping-out.

Colvin, Geoff. 2015. "Humans are underrated." *Fortune,* July 23. fortune.com/2015/07/23/humans-are-underrated/.

Cromie, William J. 2007. "Learning while we sleep and dream." *Harvard Gazette,* May 3. http://news.harvard.edu/gazette/story/2007/05/learning-while-we-sleep-and-dream/.

Gladwell, Malcolm. 2005. *Blink.* New York: Little, Brown and Company.

Gorman, Carol K. 2010. "Great Leaders Talk with Their Hands." *Forbes*, September 21. http://www.forbes.com/2010/09/21/body-language-hands-gestures-forbes-woman-leadership-communication.html.

Laporte, Nicole. 2013. "100 Most Creative People in Business 2013." *Fast Company*, May 13. http://www.fastcompany.com/3009191/most-creative-people-2013/8-bryan-cranston.

Liberman, Mattew. 2013. "Why We Are Wired to Connect." *Scientific American Magazine*, October 22. http://www.scientificamerican.com/article/why-we-are-wired-to-connect/.

Mehrabian, Albert. *Silent Messages: Implicit Communication of Emotions and Attitudes.* Belmont, CA: Wadsworth Publishing Company, 1972.

Murphy, Kate. 2014. "Psst. Look Over Here." *New York Times,* May 16. nytimes.com/2014/05/17/sunday-review/the-eyes-have-it.html?_r=0.

Musicus, Aviva, Aner Tal, and Brian Wansink. 2014. "Eyes in the Aisles: Why is Cap'n Crunch Looking Down at My Child?" *Environment & Behavior,* April 2. 10.1177/0013916514528793.

Nelson, Audrey. 2013. "Work Voice Versus Home Voice: A Women's [sic] Dilemma." *Psychology Today,* April 25. psychologytoday.com/blog/he-speaks-she-speaks/201304/work-voice-versus-home-voice-womens-dilemma.

Patel-Wilson, Terin. 2012. "The Subtle Smile." *Yale Scientific,* March 18. yalescientific.org/2012/03/the-subtle-smile-the-effect-of-smiling-and-other-non-verbal-gestures-on-gender-roles/.

"Pauses in Speech," *ScienceBlog* (blog), February 1, 2008, http://scienceblog.com/15382/pauses-in speech/#bD6szuCvUu0qMx4I.97.

Schawbel, Dan. 2013. "Sir Ken Robinson: How to Discover Your True Talents." *Forbes,* June 5. forbes.com/sites/danschawbel/2013/06/05/ sir-ken-robinson-how-to-discover-your-true-talents/.

Schilling, Diane. 2012. "10 Steps to Effective Listening." *Forbes,* November 9. forbes.com/sites/ womensmedia/2012/11/09/10-steps-to-effective-listening/.

Stewart, James B. 2015. "Ruth Porat May Be Just What Investors Think Google Needs." *New York Times,* July 23. nytimes.com/2015/07/24/business/ruth-porat-may-be-just-what-investors-think-google-needs.html?_r=0.

Treasure, Julian. 2011. "5 Ways to Listen Better." TED Talk video, July 29. https://www.bing.com/videos/s

ABOUT THE AUTHOR

If you've ever wondered, *"How can I say this so they really get it?"* you have entered into the world Cary Pfeffer knows better than most anyone on the planet.

From top executives and political leaders to television personalities and sports legends, Cary Pfeffer has provided direction and advice to make sure each of them is better at telling their story.

It was an early age when it seemed this skill was in his DNA. A national champion speech team member for three consecutive years in high school, Cary went on to a 20 year career in broadcasting as an award-winning reporter and news anchor. From there, Cary turned his attention to providing counsel on message, delivery, and audience interaction for leaders all over the world. While his life as a reporter was exciting and took him on a great journey, he will tell you his work today is what he was put here to do.

Cary lives in Phoenix, Arizona, and considers his greatest joy watching the lives of his three adult children unfold. He is also passionate about the care of people with disabilities and has been on the board of directors of Gompers in Phoenix for eight years. If you are looking for a good cause to support, go to www. GompersCenter.org.

To schedule Cary as a speaker, send a request to info@Clear-Comm.net. Cary speaks on communication and leadership across the country and is especially interested in talks which take him out of Phoenix in the months of July and August. A nice cool, beach location would be preferred . . .

To continue the dialogue, go to
www.NoAppBook.com